FROM ATTITUDE TO GRATITUDE

FROM ATTITUDE TO GRATITUDE

15 Practices for Transforming Pain into Power

BY KARI WELLS

Worth

From Attitude to Gratitude: 15 Practices for Transforming Pain into Power

Published by Worth Books, an imprint of Forefront Books.
Distributed by Simon & Schuster.

Library of Congress Control Number: 2025921399

Print ISBN: 978-1-63763-522-3
E-book ISBN: 978-1-63763 -523-0

Cover Design by Michelle Manley
Interior Design by PerfecType, Nashville, TN

Printed in the United States of America.
26 27 28 29 30 31 RR4 10 9 8 7 6 5 4 3 2 1

CONTENTS

Dear Friends,

While I've been blessed with a life rich in extraordinary experiences, I've also faced my fair share of struggles. There were long chapters of my life where I searched tirelessly for meaning, wandering the globe in pursuit of wisdom and clarity. Along the way, I've encountered spiritual teachers and guides who have shown me the deeper truths of existence.

I've meditated in the ancient temples of Thailand, drunk from the sacred springs at Lourdes, received a papal blessing at the Vatican, and prayed in cathedrals that echo centuries of faith. I've shared a quiet moment with His Holiness the Dalai Lama, dived into the deep blue waters of the ocean to swim with dolphins, climbed to the breathtaking summit of rugged peaks, and skied the pristine, powdery slopes of some of the world's most magnificent mountains.

But guess what? My life hasn't been all sunshine and roses. I come from very humble beginnings—born the youngest of seven children in the small town of Yorkshire, England, to a very strict, tough-love father and a sweet, Catholic mother who tried hard to protect us with her love and care. I grew up fast and experienced traumatic experiences early in life. And it didn't stop there—in my adult life, I've experienced traumas, had my fair share of heartbreak, and struggled with prolonged grief from losing loved ones. Like many other humans, I've had my own struggles with mental health from disordered eating, depression, and PTSD. But these difficult experiences have had a hidden reward: They've brought me closer to myself, and they've been a pathway to understanding my own mind and learning to live in a way that celebrates my whole experience and puts gratitude first, as a way of life, and transforms pain into power.

All of my life experiences—both positive and negative—have been meaningful in their own ways. They have shaped my understanding of the mind-body-spirit connection and taught me lessons I'll carry with me for the rest of my life. But here's the twist: The most profound, life-changing transformation didn't happen in some far-off temple, in the magnificence of nature, or beneath the gaze of a spiritual master. No, it happened quietly, in my own home, in a space of utter solitude. There were no grand monuments, no awe-inspiring teachers, no rituals—just me alone, in a stillness that allowed me to truly and honestly see myself for the first time.

After I discovered my true self, I finally understood the vastness of my being and the depth of the Universe inside me. When I began to see myself for who I really was, unfiltered and whole, I discovered my purpose—not something external to chase or attain, but a truth that had been with me all along, quietly waiting for me to recognize it. I had spent so many years searching the world for meaning, only to realize that everything I was looking for—wealth, power, fame—were all external illusions. What I truly needed was already within me.

This book is an invitation to share my journey with you—the lessons, the insights, and the tools I discovered that helped me unite my mind, body, and spirit. Through these pages, I hope to give you the same inspiration and clarity that transformed my life. I want to offer you the tools to move beyond the pain and challenges that weigh you down and guide you toward the peace and joy that are always within reach. This book is for anyone on a spiritual path, for anyone searching for deeper meaning, for anyone ready to find joy and gratitude in the everyday moments of life.

When I first discovered these tools, it felt as if the dragon I'd been battling my entire life—the dragon of doubt, fear, and longing—took its final breath and crumpled to the ground. And in that moment, I knew my quest had come to an end. I had *finally* found the joy and peace I'd been searching for. It is my deepest wish that you, too, find this peace. That you, too, see the beauty and magic within yourself and walk forward with renewed purpose, knowing that the path you've been seeking has always been inside you.

With love and gratitude,

Kari Wells

1

TROUBLE IN PARADISE

When You're Lying on the Ground, the Only Place to Go Is Up

The Lotus is a flower that grows in
the mud; the thicker and deeper the
mud, the more beautiful the flower.
—*Buddhist Proverb*

It was another magnificent day in Hawaii. The sun was beginning to set over Haleakalā Volcano, and pastel pink beams of light were peeking out from behind the evening clouds. The beachfront was scattered with happy couples holding hands, some already dressed for a romantic dinner, enjoying an evening cocktail. Families with young children happily played on the beach around colorful chairs and towels, relishing their precious time together and getting ready to watch nature's biggest show, the beautiful and magical sunset. People smiled, laughed, and chatted while walking along the pathway, enjoying the view of the beach, the clear evening, and the colorful, wispy clouds. It was my favorite time of day—the golden hour, when the evening light is so perfect that everything it touches is embellished with an iridescent glow, a time when all of nature can be seen blooming in full brilliance. Every time I had the opportunity to sit back and watch the incredible Maui sunset, I used it as a time to thank God and the Universe for my many blessings and to express my gratitude for yet another fantastic day spent with the people I love. However, on this particular day, I was not feeling any of my usual joy; this day, I felt quite different.

My family and I were four days into a wonderful two-week Hawaii vacation. We were living in paradise. The weather had been fabulous all week. My sweet, loving husband and our two children, who were young teenagers at the time, were happy, healthy, and enjoying the slower-paced island life—living on "Maui time," where everything seems to stand still, unlike the fast pace we were used to at home in the city. I had booked a five-star hotel, one of my favorite splurges. (I prefer to spend my money on making memories instead of accumulating more stuff.) The hotel was on the beach, in a great location, with an incredible view. For the most part, everything was impeccable. So why wasn't I feeling my usual joy?

I took a moment to settle my thoughts. Sitting there on the warm sand, listening to the gentle sound of the waves, I tried to calm my mind. I stared at the sunset in all its beauty and took a long, slow, deep breath—in through my nose, out through my mouth. I felt the warm ocean water tickle my feet as a small, flat wave brushed against my legs. I breathed in again and slowly let out another deep breath.

Breathe, just breathe, I told myself. Yet despite my efforts, I felt an oh-so-familiar feeling washing over me as warm, wet tears ran down my face. I tasted their saltiness in the corners of my mouth. In only a matter of minutes, I realized that an old companion had once again slipped in beside me. It was stealthily, silently, pressing against my chest ever so gently, making it feel tight and heavy. It made my eyes sting; it clouded my vision and began to churn the fluttering knots of anxiety in my stomach. My mind started to race in too many directions. Yes, I recognized this familiar visitor—all too well. *Depression. Melancholia. Sadness.* Call it what you will—it was an uncomfortable and unwelcome feeling.

The only thing worse than being depressed is being depressed in a tropical paradise, where everything is supposed to be perfect and you should have absolutely nothing to complain about. But that's the thing about depression—it's doesn't care who you are, where you are, or how much work you've put in to overcome it. It can still come find you.

My Struggle with Depression

I was born and raised in Yorkshire, England, where conversations about mental health were practically nonexistent.

In my family—and in much of society at the time—depression was a taboo subject, something you didn't acknowledge, not even to yourself. In my grandparents' generation, any sign of emotional struggle was seen as a character flaw, something to be "told off," pushed down, or simply ignored. You were expected to double down, toughen up, and carry on.

Despite battling internal struggles my entire life, I now reached a place where I was managing. I wasn't feeling ashamed anymore—quite the opposite, in fact. I was deeply proud of the healing I'd worked so hard to achieve. I'd come through the storm of a painful eating disorder that had consumed my teenage years and early twenties. I'd survived a childhood marked by emotional distance, shaped by a hardworking but harsh father who openly disapproved of the older sister I adored. I lived with undiagnosed ADHD that left me feeling stupid and inadequate, struggling to make sense of why school always felt so impossible. Later, a diagnosis of celiac disease shed light on the chronic exhaustion, stomach pain, and anemia that had plagued me for years. During my modeling years, my low self-esteem worsened, feeding the eating disorder that lingered well into my twenties. I endured the crushing grief of losing my beloved sister and the dark depths of postpartum depression. But through it all, I kept doing the work—bit by bit, building back my strength and reclaiming my sense of self.

After doing the hard work of healing, I finally felt mentally strong—resilient, even. And yet, just a year before taking a pivotal trip, my world was rocked once more: I was assaulted, then robbed, then betrayed by someone I trusted. It was, without question, a year from hell. But even then, I knew I was not broken. I was healing, getting better, moving on.

Society and medical professionals have come a long way in the understanding and treatment of depression. According to an article from the National Library of Medicine, early accounts of depression can be traced back to ancient civilizations, like in Mesopotamia, where it was often attributed to supernatural causes or possession by demons. In ancient Greece and Rome, physicians like Hippocrates and Galen began to view depression, or "melancholia," as a medical condition. Hippocrates believed it was caused by an imbalance of the four bodily humors, particularly an excess of black bile. During the Middle Ages, views on depression often reverted to religious interpretations, with many attributing it to sin or moral failure. Treatments included prayer, confession, and even exorcism. Women with mental illnesses were thought to be witches and frequently drowned or burned at the stake.[1]

The Enlightenment in the seventeenth and eighteenth centuries saw a shift toward understanding depression as a psychological disorder, with a focus on the mind rather than spiritual causes. Thankfully, by the nineteenth and twentieth centuries, depression began to be studied more scientifically. Sigmund Freud and other early psychiatrists explored its roots in trauma and unconscious conflicts. The twentieth century saw the development of various theories and treatments, from psychoanalysis to antidepressant medications, such as the introduction of the first tricyclic antidepressants in the 1950s and selective serotonin uptake inhibitors (SSRIs) in the 1980s.

Today depression is understood as a complex condition influenced by a combination of genetic, biological, environmental, and psychological factors. It is the most common mental health disorder worldwide today; depression and anxiety disorders affect over 40 million people in the US alone and affect women at double the rate of men. One in four women will suffer from depression or anxiety at some point in their lives. Each year, there are breakthroughs that reveal the causes and treatment of depression, and thankfully, there is now a wide range of treatments available, including psychotherapy, medication, and lifestyle changes.[2]

We now know that depression is not in any way a weakness of character, but the stigma stubbornly persists in our society. Some individuals feel ashamed about their depression, mistakenly believing they should be able to overcome it with willpower or simply "snap out of it." However, most of us now understand that depression is a lot more complex than that; it's a true biological condition affecting the brain and its imbalances. That's what I was feeling on that beach in Hawaii. I wasn't new to mental health struggles; I knew depression all too well and had, in fact, spent much of my adult life devoted to healing myself. But this overwhelming feeling had a new flavor. I'd done so much emotional work to heal from what had been one of the toughest years of my adult life, but lingering PTSD and grief still occasionally rose up to threaten my joy.

My Year from Hell

With trauma, PTSD, and several huge life setbacks, the year had been a challenging one for me. I was assaulted at gunpoint, was a victim of identity theft, and was betrayed by a close business associate whom I considered family. I'd thought the events of that year were behind me. I really thought I was okay, but boy was I wrong. Trauma has a way of surprising you when you least expect it. I had been unbelievably busy with my career, my kids, their school activities, my marriage, my family and friends, and the several businesses I was running. This Hawaiian vacation was the first time in a long time I'd had a moment to just stop and relax, so it was no wonder that all the memories—and the subsequent feeling of depression—came flooding back. Thinking about all the things I'd recently endured—one October night in particular, the night of the assault—threatened to crowd out the joyful mindset I'd worked so hard to attain.

Back then our family was living in a beautiful Atlanta neighborhood in a home my husband and I had built in a gorgeous forest surrounded by majestic old trees and wildlife. It had been our home for twelve years, and I loved spending time there, hanging out with my children, making sure they finished their homework, preparing dinner, and spending quality time with my husband. It was a place where I felt safe. On this October evening, I'd had a stressful day and desperately needed some me time, so I booked a relaxing mani-pedi at my favorite salon. My husband was watching a movie with the kids, so it was easy for me to slip out for an hour or so. I booked the last appointment of the day, knowing the salon would be slow and I could catch up on emails and texts in peace.

I drove to the salon, where I enjoyed my hour of pampering and catching up on correspondence. When my nails and toes were done, I headed to the counter to settle my bill and made some small talk with the woman at the front desk, remarking on how dark it was outside: "Wow, it must be late. Am I the last person here?" She smiled and assured me I wasn't: "No, we have one more client in the back." I noticed a young woman who was still getting her nails done in a quiet corner at the back of the salon.

I paid my bill and pulled out some cash from my wallet then walked to the back of the salon to give each of the nail technicians some tip money. As I turned around to leave, two men entered the salon with large guns pointed directly at us, screaming, "Everyone get down!" It was like something out of a movie, and at first my mind thought it must be a Halloween stunt, but the men stormed into the salon, guns blazing, and locked the doors behind them. I froze in place as they walked over and stopped on either side of me with their guns drawn, pointing toward my head.

"Okay, this is going down!" one of them yelled. The young women who worked at the nail salon began screaming at the top of their lungs, attempting to run to the back of the salon.

"No one fucking move!" yelled one of the armed robbers as he fired his gun toward the women who were running. "Nobody is leaving this place! So get the fuck down!"

Everyone froze. Time stood still.

I made a mental note that the gunmen were not wearing masks. I could clearly see their faces, and they could see mine. This, I realized, was not a good sign. Anyone who has ever watched any kind of a heist movie knows that robbers never allow themselves to be recognized, unless they plan on killing their victims. No armed robber wants to leave behind any witnesses. This was blatantly clear to me, yet at the same time, all my senses were dulled. I was in a surreal state, not knowing what was real, what to focus on, or what action to take. But some part of me *did* know at that moment, with every cell of my being, that my actions would define the outcome of this situation.

Knowing that I needed to calm myself, I took a couple of deep breaths. I watched one of the men walk behind the counter and violently hit the manager in the face with his gun. The place was in chaos, with everyone screaming and crying and the gunmen stomping back and forth trying to round everyone up at gunpoint. One of them forced the manager to open the cash drawer as he held the gun to his head. The robber then hit him over the back of the head with his gun. Another robber pulled out the cash drawer and threw it to the floor. Piles of cash spilled onto the carpet as it crashed down. They hastily gathered as much cash as they could in a wild scramble as they continued to threaten the staff. Then they began grabbing the women's purses. One of the salon staff grabbed her client's purse, I assume to prevent the robbers from taking it, or maybe she planned to hand it to him, since he was brandishing a gun near her head. But he kicked her in the face hard, like he was kicking a football, and she fell motionless to the floor.

I was astonished at the violence that was being shown. I'd always assumed that if you handed the robbers the goods, you would be spared, but this was apparently not the case.

I could see the woman's body lying on the floor, her face swollen and bloody. This situation had just become a whole lot more serious. It was pandemonium now. I could hear people sobbing, but I was still frozen in place. Because I didn't want to be shot, or draw any attention to myself, I removed my diamond engagement ring and hid it in my underwear when the robbers weren't looking, hoping this would make me less of a target.

My heart was beating so loudly in my chest, I could feel it through the screaming and yelling. I stood silently in a surreal trance with my arms raised above my head in the surrender position. I did not want to get down on the floor; the reception counter stood between me and the robbers, and I feared they would think I was hiding behind it. Not wanting to do anything to alarm them, I stood perfectly still, frozen, my arms raised high, hoping they would ignore me.

Suddenly, I felt a sharp and intense pain at the back of my head. "Get down, bitch!" one of the robbers screamed as he aggressively pistol-whipped me. My ears were ringing as I crashed to the ground, my head smashing into the porcelain tiles with an intense force. Everything went black. I tried to open my eyes, but pain flooded through my head, face, and neck like a steel spike. I lay on the ground, hurt and confused, trying to gain my composure.

My brain raced as I tried to process the reality of the situation and the choices I was faced with. I could see the exit, and my car was just on the other side of it, but I didn't know if I could make it in my injured state, and honestly, I was too afraid to make a run for it. I knew that from that moment on, every action, every slight move, even every facial expression, could determine whether I lived or died.

My thoughts immediately went to my children—how young they were, how they still had their entire lives ahead of them, how much they still needed me. *I must get home,* I silently told myself. *I must survive this—my kids still need me to take care of them. I can't die here, not now. There's no way I am going down like this.* The lights seemed to dim, probably from my head injury, and everything seemed blurry. At this point, I was only aware that I had intense pain in my head, and my elbow had a deep cut that was bleeding profusely.

I slowly got to my knees, trying to gather my composure. There was broken glass all around me, and I felt it under my skin. My vision was hazy; the lights in the room seemed fuzzy and dim. The pain I was feeling was so intense that it forced me to stay on my knees, bent over like a bowing monk. I could still hear screaming and crying amid the scuffle.

From my place on the floor behind the reception counter, all I could see was the blur of the ground, the feet of the gunmen, and the body of the girl near me. I began to carefully crawl along the ceramic floor tiles that were now covered with cash and broken glass. Amid the chaos, I heard one of the robbers shout, "That white bitch is on the phone!"

All the employees in the salon were Asian, and the only other client still there was a young Black woman, so I knew he was talking about me. My thoughts were shattered by the heavy sound of feet stomping toward me. My heart stopped with fear, and I froze, still on my hands and knees, staring at the ground. I prayed I would become invisible, like a child playing hide-and-seek, and that the man headed my way wouldn't notice me crouching on the floor.

But that was not the case.

The stomping stopped, along with the beating of my heart, as one of the gunmen approached me, his boots appearing in my line of vision. He forcefully pushed the cold metal gun against the back of my head, forcing my face to press up against the ceramic floor tile.

"Are you on the phone, bitch?" he screamed into my ear. "I will fucking kill you, bitch! I will fucking kill you! Are you on the phone?! Are you on the phone?!" He shouted this over and over.

I stretched my hands across the floor, lying flat so he could see I wasn't on the phone. "I am *not* on the phone!" I tried to yell in a broken voice. I closed my eyes and thought once again of my children and how much they still needed me. I was crippled with pain and confusion, and I felt completely powerless, but from some deep place within me, I told myself, *No matter what, I am going to do whatever it takes to make it out of here alive.*

This was not at all how I'd always imagined I would react in a situation like this. I never thought that I would feel so impotent, so helpless. But as Mike Tyson so eloquently put it, in the press conferences before one of his big fights, "Everyone has a plan until you get punched in the mouth."

Finally, after a period of silence—I had no idea how long it lasted—I heard someone shout, "They're gone!" I rose to a standing position amid broken glass and overturned furniture. The staff were now sprinting toward the back door. I ran barefoot through the shattered glass and random belongings that now littered the floor, following everyone out of the back of the store. It was pitch dark outside, but I could see several staff members hiding in their cars. I saw one young woman alone in her car, and without thinking, I opened the passenger side door and got in. It seemed like a good place to hide. She was crying uncontrollably. I instructed her to get down onto the floor, so that we couldn't be seen from the outside. We both crouched down, hidden from view and counting the seconds until the car's automatic entry lights slowly faded. At this point, we didn't know where the gunmen were, and fear was still running rampant through our bodies. For what seemed like forever, we waited and waited in the car, trying to will ourselves invisible. Suddenly, we heard sirens—the police were on their way, and although I was relieved to hear this, I was still petrified and felt battered and bruised.

I was fortunate to walk away from that situation with only a concussion, a large bruise on my forehead, a lump at the back of my skull, an elbow laceration, and multiple contusions. Although I looked like Worf from Star Trek with my swollen forehead, I knew I'd been extremely lucky to have gotten out of that nail salon with my life.

When my husband arrived to pick me up, he couldn't believe the state I was in. Looking at my face, he was shocked at how calm I seemed, considering I'd just been assaulted at gunpoint. He kept asking me *why* I was not screaming and crying, but my response came out calm and calculated, and I appeared to be in a dreamlike state. Looking back, this was clearly because of the shock I was in. My husband is a surgeon, trained in trauma, yet when he heard what was happening to me, he ran out of the house in a frantic state, leaving the children home alone. He wanted to get me out of there as soon as possible after he arrived, but the police insisted I stay for what seemed like hours of questioning.

When I arrived home, still in a daze, I hugged and kissed my family like never before. And yet from that night on, I couldn't sleep for weeks from the fear. The gunmen had taken my belongings, including my car keys and house keys. Would they be able to determine where I lived? I felt that my life in Atlanta, in the dream home we had so carefully built, would never feel safe again—and that I would never feel the same way I did before this life-changing event happened.

This traumatic event truly capped what had already been an insanely sucky year—one that had begun with a phone call, out of the blue, from a credit agency. The female voice on the other end of the phone told me that due to my increased spending and the many large purchases I had recently made to my store account, she wanted to know if I would like to increase the amount of my credit. She informed me that even though I'd spent the maximum the store credit card would allow, she was happy to offer me an increased limit. I had absolutely no idea what she was taking about. What store? What spending? What purchases? My heart began racing as I listened to her list off the many items I'd bought. I explained to her that I didn't even have an account at that store, suggesting that she must be mistaken. These were not my charges; they must have been someone else's.

As she explained more details to me, I realized someone must have opened an account in my name. I knew it hadn't been me because I had spent the last three weeks super busy at work and hadn't had any time to shop. It was slowly becoming clear that I was the victim of identity theft. I spent the remainder of the afternoon speaking to identity theft experts. Together we discovered that five store credit accounts had been opened in my name in the past month.

As anyone who has experienced identity theft can tell you, it takes a long time to recover from it, and it's something that most definitely does not just go away on its own. It is, in fact, a nightmare that involves weeks and weeks of phone calls, letters, police reports, and detective work. As I spoke to several experts from various credit agencies, I learned of the five separate accounts at five different department stores that had recently been opened in my name, all of which had excessive spending and balances of over eighteen thousand dollars. The person who had stolen my identity had gone on a variety of shopping sprees at my expense, one for almost fifteen thousand dollars. She'd bought expensive watches, designer purses, high-end jewelry, and gift cards. I'd never even visited some of the stores where she'd shopped. I spent the next six months getting a crash course in identity theft and doing everything I could to clear my name and protect my credit. The maze of paperwork and red tape required to prove my innocence felt endless, and the process was exhausting. After many shopping sprees at the luxury stores all over metro Atlanta and the surrounding neighborhoods, my identity thief was finally caught. Her downfall came when she tried peddling the high-end stolen goods online.

This was not a woman who was desperate to feed her family; she was not buying baby food or diapers or children's clothing. She was simply looking for an easy way to make money, and I was her victim. Videos posted online by the authorities showed that she was using other people's credit to furnish her lavish lifestyle. She was finally caught when her (so-called) friend turned her in for the reward money that was offered by crime stoppers. Sadly, because she was a repeat offender, she is now getting all her expenses paid—in prison.

Identity theft is not something that just goes away on its own; for many victims, it ruins their lives. It left me feeling exposed, vulnerable, and violated. I'd always had so much trust in humanity and rarely doubted people's honesty, so the most challenging part for me was that I became more cynical.

A few weeks after recovering from my identity theft, I was hit with another kind of betrayal. We discovered a trusted employee who had worked for my husband's medical practice for twelve long years—someone we had treated like a family member—had been stealing from us for quite some time. This person ran our business. She knew our children, our parents, and our Social Security numbers, and we trusted her completely.

Because we considered her a friend, we'd welcomed her into our lives. A couple of times over the years, she had come to us in times of need, and each time, we helped her, going above and beyond what a regular employer would do. We gave her money to pay off her loans when she got into debt and even helped her navigate personal family issues and her problems with the IRS.

We *never* thought she would steal from us, especially because we always had her back. Plus, she had a successful career with us and was earning an excellent salary. It was a tough time for our family when we discovered her many lies, deceptions, and betrayals. The situation was so severe that it almost caused our business to close. This betrayal hit me the hardest because she was someone whom I admired and trusted.

Yes, this had been a very challenging year for me. But as I sat on that beautiful beach in Maui, feeling the warm sand between my toes, I was determined that I would not be defeated by these challenges. There's an old saying that "when you are already on the floor, the only way you can go is up," and this was my plan. *Up.*

From Breakdown Comes Breakthrough

Hearing a flock of seagulls cawing as they flew above and feeling the warm sand around me, I remembered why I'd come out to the shore: I needed to once again find healing. What a year it had been! And now that I had been given space and time to think, the negative memories came pouring back into my mind. The beach was clearing, and the sun had gone down, but still I sat there with the waves tickling my feet, feeling a deep sadness. Was I feeling sorry for myself? Was that it? Then I remembered one last thing that had happened to me just a few days previously. Maybe this actually had been the straw that broke the camel's back. Some say that bad luck comes in threes, but this was the *fourth* terrible thing that had happened to me that year. It was beginning to feel like a dark cloud was following me around.

When we'd arrived at our beautiful Maui hotel, I discovered that my purse was missing, along with a bag containing my favorite jewelry: a diamond necklace, a gold cuff bracelet, and a few other pieces. It was not about the cost of the stolen items, because I believe that if something can be solved with time or money, it's not really a problem, only a setback. What hurt the most was that every piece of jewelry in my stolen purse had extreme sentimental value. What the hell was happening in my life?

I laid back on the sand and stretched out at far as I could. The sun had gone down, and I stared at the evening sky. What was the Universe trying to show me? What was my spiritual guide trying to teach me? Why was all of this happening to me, or rather, as I prefer to think, why was this happening *for* me?

I thought of all the times in my life I'd survived whatever was thrown at me, and I'd picked myself up, dusted myself off, and moved on. I'd overcome a difficult childhood. I'd started supporting myself financially at the age of seventeen. I'd moved to America as an immigrant at the age of twenty-two, with only a few thousand dollars, a pair of skis, and a suitcase. I thought about all the things I'd been through in my life. And I knew that feeling sorry for myself would *never* get me anywhere.

No matter what cards life deals you, feeling sorry for yourself is never a useful tool—only a self-defeating long-term strategy. Yes, you must allow yourself some time to mourn, to heal, and to be kind to yourself, but at some point, no matter what the circumstances, you *must* decide to accept your fate and come to terms with it; otherwise, you will remain stuck inside your pain for the rest of your life, always stunted and lacking the ability to grow and learn from it. Believe me, I haven't always found this easy—especially with some of my more difficult struggles—but with acceptance as the first step, time and time again, I have come out wiser on the other side of life's most painful experiences.

It was on that beach in Maui, replaying so many painful experiences and difficult emotions, where overwhelming negative feelings threatened to take me to a low place, testing me yet again, just when I thought I'd healed. I decided it was time to ask myself some deeper questions: *How did I get here? Why am I feeling so terribly low? Why are the spiritual tools that I've learned along the way not working for me? What am I doing wrong?*

In the process of asking myself these questions—in getting real with myself—I realized it was my journey that had led me *here.* A journey that had begun a long time ago, marked with a heartbreaking grief that I can only describe as "walking through the Pain Caves," which you'll learn more about in the next chapter. Grief was my entry point, my gateway to a beautiful path of deep spiritual healing. Everyone has their own journey, their own challenges, setbacks, and struggles. But the same transformative tools that have helped me through my darkest times can also help you when the so-called sh*t hits the fan. Even when trouble comes calling for you in paradise, you always have a choice and when you are lying on the floor, the only place to go is up. You must choose to go "up" when life brings you down.

2

A WALK THROUGH THE PAIN CAVES

You Have to Feel It to Heal It

The only way out is through.
—*Robert Frost*

For most of my life, I have tried to live by a simple yet powerful philosophy: *Everything happens for a reason, and that reason is to benefit me.* I intentionally chose this philosophy so I could always be in charge of my choices, because I never wanted to feel like a victim of my circumstances. When I'm faced with adversity, this philosophy helps me process my thoughts and emotions and ensures I never feel powerless. These words of wisdom work wonders when things are going well, but when life suddenly changes or circumstances send you into a downward spiral, maintaining a positive outlook can be extremely difficult. However, holding steadfast to this philosophy can be a lighthouse that will guide you through dark times. This following story is not told to invite sympathy, but only to remind you that heartbreak can be the very forge where both strength and resilience are born and that out of darkness comes light.

It was 1995, I was living in Aspen, a beautiful ski town in the heart of the Colorado Rockies. I was spending a ski season getting in as many "powder days" as possible and feeling extremely lucky to have this time and experience, doing all I could to make the most of it. Aspen is famous for its four majestic ski mountains, epic vistas, designer stores, fabulous hotels and restaurants, and of course, world-class skiing. It attracts people from all over the globe for an array of experiences that cannot be duplicated anywhere else. It is truly a magical place, bringing year-round visitors for winter skiing, summer festivals, and the most spectacular fall colors.

One winter night, as I was enjoying my new life in Aspen and feeling unstoppable, my phone rang. I was surprised to hear my mother's voice on the other end. My parents live in England, so with the seven-hour time difference, I quickly figured out it must have been around five o'clock in the morning there. I had just returned home from an elegant Christmas party, and I was feeling extremely jolly from the delicious champagne I'd freely imbibed for most of the night. I was in my twenties and living life to the fullest, making the most of each moment. My priorities were working, skiing, saving money, and having as much fun as possible.

"Hi, Mum," I answered with a smile. "What are you doing up so early?"

My mother paused, her voice soft and fragile on the other end of the phone. "Well, my darling, I am so sorry to say that we have some bad news I need to tell you."

"What is it, Mum?"

"It's your sister . . . She died tonight."

"What—what are you saying?" I replied, shocked.

"She died on the way to the hospital tonight," she sobbed. "I am so sorry to have to tell you over the phone, my love, and I wish I could have told you in person."

Shock can make you do strange things. I could not take in the words my mother was telling me; my brain simply refused to accept them. I grabbed a pen and notepad that sat on my desk and asked her to repeat what she was telling me so I could write it down.

Jackie DEAD, I wrote on the paper.

My poor, sweet mother had just left the hospital after saying goodbye to her dead child—my sister—and now she was having to deal with the task of telling her other children the horrible news. And there I was, asking her to repeat it over and over because my brain could not accept the words. My sister was dead due to an accidental overdose; she was only twenty-nine years old.

It felt like the world as I knew it had ended.

I made the arduous journey home to England to be with my family for Jackie's funeral and the excruciating week of mourning. It was the first time I had ever seen my strong and stern military-trained father cry like a child. After he picked up Angela, my older sister, and me from the airport in Manchester, he had to pull the car over because he'd begun to sob uncontrollably. We had never seen him this way, and we were both in complete shock. To see him now, so fragile and broken, shattered our hearts even more.

At home, my mother was holding herself together as best she could, trying to conceal her own heartbreak in order to reassure the rest of us that everything was going to be okay. Mum always thought about the feelings of other people first. She was a stoic, saintly, and beautiful soul; she wanted to be as strong as she could for me, my dad, my grandmother, and her children and grandchildren.

But we could see that she, too, was broken.

Loss leaves you with a profound emptiness and hurts like a deep ache, one that feels eternal. To lose a child is a pain no parent should ever have to endure; you break down, you break open, and the rawness of your grief is wounding. It seeps into every fiber of your being.

The Darkness of the Pain Caves

I mourned deeply for my sister. She was my best friend growing up. We shared our entire childhood, secrets, laughter, and stories. And now she was gone forever. I felt like the bottom had fallen out from my world, like my life would never be the same—and *I* would never be the same. I was staring at the entryway of what I call the Pain Caves, and all I could see was darkness.

Elisabeth Kübler-Ross wrote in her 1969 book *On Death and Dying* that there are five stages of grief: denial, anger, bargaining, depression, and acceptance.

In the first stage, **denial**, there is a bit of grace in that we cannot fully register the total pain, shock, and disbelief over our loss in one moment or one day, so the pain is spread out over time to help us cope with it.

Anger, the second stage, is our natural reaction to loss, whether it's anger at the cause of death, the deceased, the god of your religion, yourself, or the facts of the matter.

Then comes the third stage: **bargaining**. This often stems from guilt, with bargaining after a loss typically involving "If only . . ." and "What if . . ." statements that are focused on the regrets of what you did or didn't do before the loss.

The fourth stage is **depression**, or acute sadness, when the immense loss begins to affect us more deeply—and affect our entire lives. Sometimes the sadness feels as if it will last forever. We can also withdraw from life in this stage, wondering if it's worth living without our loved one.

The final stage is **acceptance**. Acceptance doesn't mean you're okay with the person being gone. It just means that you now accept the new reality of your life.

For me, the stages of grief didn't come in order. It is not like you can carefully check each box step by step, like completing a work or school assignment; it is not like you can happily move on to the next stage with an end target in sight. The stages tend to come in disorganized waves, pummeling you and beating you down as, lost in an ocean of grief and despair, you struggle not to drown. Losing my sister so young and so tragically made the bargaining stage last the longest for me. I bargained with the world, bargained with everything I believed in, and bargained with myself, painfully living from moment to moment with the endless questioning of "What if?"

During the next few months, I would often cry myself to sleep, curling up in a tiny ball, waiting and hoping for the earth to swallow me up, praying for the gaping hole in my soul to heal. I would awaken with tears running down my cheeks before I was even fully awake. And when I finally opened my eyes, the sad reality of my situation would hit me full force.

My days were spent remembering every conversation I could remember having with Jackie, every comment I had made during her years of addiction. I would recall the painful visits when she was in a rehab facility, the times when she was locked away in the hope of recovery from her addiction. I replayed so many moments, hoping she knew my motive had always been love and not judgment. My sister had suffered a great deal in her short time on this earth and had been so fragile. It had often been difficult to know what to say to her, and I'd hated myself for not being mature enough to understand what she needed and, ultimately, for not having been able to save her. There were many years when I'd been so self-absorbed in my teenage life that I was unaware of the extent of Jackie's suffering. I felt like I had failed her on so many occasions, yet I was a child, and at that time, I didn't have the tools or the maturity to cope with the situation.

Outside, the sunlight is shining brightly,
its light casting a warm glow through the kitchen window;
inside, my heart is still, and a deep pain radiates through my chest.
Like frostbitten fingers from an arctic winter, it stings bitterly!
The sorrow overcomes me and comfortably rests within me.
It has lived here before and feels at home.
Sinking deeply, like a blanket of snow, it becomes me.
The melancholia deepens in my fractured heart,
Why do we hold on to things with such blind attachment?
Everything but our memories will be stripped from us in the end.
My path is the path of my destiny, a path no mortal can change.
I ask for a miracle . . . but I fear I have no favor.
I cried a river of tears, deep like the ocean,
My heart felt the ice that had now settled in.
I will shake off the memories like dust in the wind.
I will smile again . . .

—A Walk Through the Darkness by Kari Wells

Grief, the Great Teacher

When I moved out of my childhood home at the tender age of seventeen, my parents allowed me to go live with Jackie. It seemed like a good idea at the time, but my poor parents had no idea about her addiction and they were doing the best they could with the limited information they had. My sister's very strained relationship with our father had deteriorated tremendously, and her living at home under his watchful and ever-critical eye was becoming a nightmare for everyone. The one who suffered the most next to Jackie was our poor mother, who was always in the middle of trying to defuse arguments and hold the family together.

For quite some time, Jackie's relationship with our father had not been great; in short, he wanted her to be someone she wasn't. The disharmony between them arose from his military strictness and his unaddressed trauma from being a child during the Second World War. His austerity clashed strongly with her wild and free spirit. They tried to understand each other, but their viewpoints were worlds apart.

I was happy to leave home at age seventeen, as was Jackie, who was four years my senior. No longer under the military-like rule of our disciplinarian father, we felt relieved to escape the pressure. Looking back, it probably was not the best decision to allow a seventeen-year-old to take care of her twenty-one-year-old, drug-addicted sister, but assuming she was protecting us, my sweet mother thought it was for the best that we move away from the constant battles with our father, who sometimes resorted to violence. This, my mother believed, was her last shot at giving us a chance at a more peaceful life with some freedom, away from my father's constant scrutiny and disapproval of Jackie's punk-rock style, complete with dyed blue hair.

So my sister and I moved into a two-bedroom apartment in the city of Leeds, which we quickly discovered had a lot more going on than our small town. I began working full-time and supporting myself financially. My very first job was at the Clinique cosmetics counter at a high-end department store, and I was elated. I'd lied about my age in order to get the job, but this was back in the days when companies were unable to properly check your identification. Employers mainly cared that you were a good fit for the job and you worked hard.

As a part of my training, I was sent away to work in London at the Clinique UK headquarters. It was a dream come true, and I loved every minute of it. Being in London made me feel so grown-up—traveling back and forth, going to the tube stations, and staying in a posh hotel, all expenses paid, were very new experiences to me. I felt on top of the world, having the glamour of the upscale cosmetics industry and the luxurious London lifestyle at my fingertips, and I immersed myself in all of it.

When my training ended, I took the train from London to Leeds, feeling so proud of myself. I was dressed in my cute white Clinique uniform, my hair up in a bun, my face expertly made up, and my luggage full of makeup and skin care samples. I couldn't wait to tell Jackie all about my trip. I took the elevator up to our apartment, still grinning, but when I tried to open the door, it was locked. I knocked, but nobody answered.

I assumed my sister wasn't home, so I reached into my purse to grab my keys. When I finally got into the apartment, I walked down the hall, past my sister's room, and then I saw Jackie slumped down at the side of her bed, covered in blood.

The blood was coming from her wrists; she did not appear to be conscious. It was clear to me that she had taken something to put her into an altered state. I rushed to my sister's bed and began tearing up her bedsheets (my mother had taught me a lot of things, one of which was how to stop bleeding in an emergency situation). I bandaged Jackie's wrists and did what I could to stop the bleeding, tying ripped pieces of cotton around her wounds while I waited for what seemed like an eternity for the ambulance to come.

When the paramedics arrived, my sister was rushed to the emergency room. The medical staff stitched up her wrists and pumped her stomach to remove whatever drug she had taken. I spent what seemed like forever in the ER waiting room, not knowing if she would make it. Around midnight, the doctor came out to talk to me and congratulated me for saving my sister's life. I was grateful and relieved that her life had been spared, never imagining that only a few years later she would be gone.

The Gift of Grief

After Jackie's death, I surfaced from my grief a totally different person—older, tougher, more resilient, yet more broken. I was much more realistic about life and its value. Could it be that I'd been broken *open*? As the years passed and the intensity of my grieving began to lessen, I slowly began to realize that I was no longer the same young, naive, self-absorbed teenager that I was before my sister died. I became a new person, and I had a whole new, incredible gift: *empathy* and *compassion*. This was a priceless gift that my sister had bequeathed to me the day she died, but it took me years to fully recognize that it was indeed a gift.

I had not known it at the time, but as I reflected on who Jackie had been, I finally understood that she was a beautiful soul, full of kindness and love. She had compassion for everyone. She sometimes spent time with the homeless, the sick, the destitute, and the people society generally turns a blind eye to. She lived by a mantra she often reminded me of: "Never judge a person until you have walked a mile in their shoes." It may sound cliché, but it's a profound message that I still live by.

Although I did not know it during my years of heavy grieving, I had been profoundly and permanently impacted by Jackie's death and her legacy. For the first time, I really reflected on who I wanted to become as a person. The choices I would make and the trajectory of my life from that point on would never be the same.

Jackie taught me about kindness, acceptance, humility, tolerance, and the importance of not judging others. She taught me to be brave, to care for animals, and to laugh and cry without fear of judgment. She taught me to value time spent with others. Even though she had so little, she taught me about money—that it cannot buy happiness or even one more second of time. Most of all, she taught me about love.

When I finally rebuilt my world, I began to look at life quite differently. I realized I cared much less about the superficial and shallow things that had entertained me so much in the past. No longer did I want to waste time on worthless friendships or people with little depth. I started to form more meaningful relationships, and I began doing more in-depth work on myself, growing personally and spiritually.

Pain Is a Love

Grief has visited me more than once in my life. Since the tragic loss of my sister Jackie, there have been several other times when I suffered deeply—after the death of my mother (which just about killed me), after the death of some dear friends, and during the stressful and challenging months of my husband's open-heart surgery.

Those low points in life, when you feel like your whole world is slowly falling apart right in front of you, are never fun to go through, to say the least, but if you have some tools in your back pocket, you can pull yourself out of them. I have learned that there is a way to use *any* pain I endure as a pathway to spiritual growth and education. If you choose to open yourself to the beauty of life's wisdom (even when it comes in the disguise of pain, loss, and tragedy), then you always have a choice how to respond. Once you are broken, you can either stay broken and shut down, or you can break open and reach the inside of your heart, to discover your true spirit, to find out exactly who you are.

When going through grief, whether it's after the death of a loved one, the end of a relationship, the loss of a friendship, or the conclusion of a career, the first thing you must do is to accept it. Accept the fact that you are indeed going through sorrow or grief. This may seem obvious, but the simple act of acceptance alone can be a daily reminder to be extra kind to yourself. Allow yourself to sit in your grief, accepting the pain and the rawness of it.

This might sound counterintuitive, but grief is pure love. Grief is your connection to that person you still love but can no longer be with. Sit with it, sit with them, feel the love, and feel the connection.

You may be going through grief right now as you read this book, and if so, my heart goes out to you. You may be feeling a pain you have never felt before, and it may seem like it will last forever. But *trust me*—the pain will not always be this raw. There is a little sweetness in sorrow, where you know and fully understand the depth of your love, and you understand the love you have lost. But here's the kicker: That love is within *you*. When a heart is broken from any type of loss—whether that's the loss of a relationship, a friendship, a career, a dream, or a beloved pet—when the walls of protection around your fragile heart are entirely dismantled, there is only love left inside. The pain we feel is our love. It is pure, it is raw, and it is beautiful.

Don't be afraid to walk through your personal Pain Caves, you may feel you are scraping your fingers to the bone, trying to find any way out. But just *stop*! Take a deep breath. Put your hand on your heart and feel it beating. Breathe! Try to breathe in so deeply that you fill your stomach with air. Then let it all go—in one large *whoosh!* Repeat these actions over and over until you feel a bit calmer.

Try to smile as you keep your hands on your heart and feel that love.

Don't be afraid to sit with this feeling for a while and just accept it.

Hold your heart as you breathe in and out, and through the pain.

Try to feel the *love* as you hold yourself in that space.

It may be days, it may be weeks, it may be months, and for some, it may even be years, but eventually, you will glimpse the sunshine peeking through the opening of the Pain Caves. You will be able to *choose* to walk out toward the light, to feel the sunshine as you finally step outside. You will feel its glow warming your tired mind and body. And one day, when you look back at that challenging time, you will realize you have left the darkness behind and a space for *love* has opened in your heart—and that LOVE will be with you for the rest of your days.

3

THE VICTIM MENTALITY

See Yourself as a Survivor and Move Forward with Your Life

It is not what happens to you.
It is how you react to it.
—*Epictetus*

Everybody makes choices in life—every day, every moment, with everything we do. Whether we're conscious of it or not, we are all making choices and decisions in every moment of our lives. Right now, you are making the choice to read this book and perhaps to make some self-improvements.

Even when we think we have no choice, we still make choices. When faced with problems and adversity, we can choose to be happy, sad, or angry. We can choose to take action or ignore what's happening. We can choose to take things personally or let things roll off our backs. These choices won't always be easy—especially choices like deciding to be happy in a negative situation or letting things that normally bother us just roll off our backs—but we do have the choice about how we choose to react to our circumstances. Life is a series of choices, after all. And remember this: 10 percent of life's suffering is our actual circumstances, and 90 percent of our suffering is how we choose to react to it!

Once you realize you have a choice, a tiny door will appear or a small window of opportunity will await, and it will gradually open to a more expansive way of thinking until you are eventually able to leave the victim mentality behind. At some point, no matter what circumstances are bringing you down and preventing you from moving forward, you have to make the conscious decision to *get over it* and move your life forward.

The Victim Mentality

A victim mentality is an acquired personality trait in which a person tends to identify as a victim of the negative actions of others. It is a pernicious thought process where one frequently or constantly perceives oneself as a "victim." In some cases, those with a victim mentality have been the recipients of wrongdoing by others or have otherwise suffered misfortune through no fault of their own. The term is also used for the tendency to blame one's misfortunes on somebody else's misdeeds, which I like to call *victimism*.

According to *Psychology Today*, a victim mentality is first developed or learned from family dysfunction and abusive situations during childhood. Sometimes criminals engage in this type of thinking, believing themselves to be moral individuals who engage in crime only as a reaction to an immoral world, often feeling that authorities are unfairly singling them out for punishment. With a victim mentality, the person lives a life where they consistently see themselves as someone who has been wronged and therefore, they feel powerless over the choices they make and the situations they allow themselves to be in.[3]

I once read a story about a man who suffered terrible burns all over his body during the Vietnam War when a phosphorous grenade exploded in his hand, leaving him disfigured. After the injury, he almost didn't survive and endured unbearable pain and suffering. Through it all, in every dark day and every setback of his life, he made the decision to not let his circumstances define him. He could have given in to a victim mentality, but he *decided* to move away from that limiting, stuck mindset. He empowered himself, took agency over his own life, and went on to write best-selling books about his experience. Now Dave Roever is a well-known motivational speaker who inspires others through his story and reaches out to those facing challenges related to war, trauma, and addiction.

When addressing audiences, Roever tells people about his journey to finding happiness and fulfillment and discovering meaning in his life. He tells the story of how he met a woman and fell in love, jokingly sharing that the one thing he never had to worry about was his wife marrying him for his looks. Though it may sound self-deprecating, it is an empowering way of thinking, turning pain into purpose and even being able to find humor in one's story as a way of conveying to those listening that each and every one of us is worthy of love and the life we desire. The moment I read Dave's story, I felt a spark of joy. It solidified the feeling that had been a growing seedling inside me as I recovered from grief: It is not what happens to you but how you decide to process what happens. We all have that choice—all of us!

Wisdom Through Hardship

What we choose can define the outcome of our lives and the content of our happiness. It can determine whether we triumph or fail, whether we live in anger and sorrow or in acceptance and gratitude. Many people who have suffered great pain will tell you that although they may wish it had never happened, they see the *gift* it has left them with. They realize how much they have learned on their spiritual journey and how much more peace they now have in their lives. They will tell you that they actually feel better emotionally and that their relationships with others (and with themselves) have greatly improved. When hardship happens, wisdom awaits us, wisdom we can take into all areas of our lives.

Those of us who allow hardship and pain to change us are granted those gifts. It's the silver lining in what many would perceive as a dark cloud. When we allow ourselves to break open, as opposed to breaking down (victim mentality), we often discover an aspect of ourselves that never would have surfaced otherwise. We discover great courage, unbelievable strength, and remarkable resilience. Sometimes, when things are falling apart, they are actually falling into place. This is certainly what I noticed happening in my life in the wake of my sister's death.

Will you continue to feel like a victim of your past suffering, or will you decide to be the victor? Will you decide today not to focus on your suffering but instead focus on the wisdom you have gained from it? The Austrian neurologist, psychiatrist, and Holocaust survivor Viktor Frankl wrote in his 1947 book *Man's Search for Meaning* about his survival experience: "Everything can be taken from a man, but one thing: the last of the human freedoms—to choose one's attitude in any given set of circumstances, to choose one's way."[4] Decades after it was written, this powerful message still lives on. Every day of our lives, at every moment, we have a chance to decide how we will respond to our difficulties and tribulations.

When we consciously or unconsciously choose to adopt a victim mentality, we blame others for our problems and leave ourselves powerless. But if other people are in charge of our problems, then they are also in charge of the solutions to our problems. In other words, we are choosing to allow another person or event to be responsible for our happiness. I found this to be a very simple yet life-changing discovery. You may have heard people say, or perhaps you yourself have said, "I will be happy if he/she/it/they would just ___________." If you are still blaming someone or something else for your circumstances or your unhappiness, I am sorry to break it to you (drumroll, please) . . . *you* are playing the victim!

In playing the victim, you have chosen to give away all your power. But it doesn't have to be that way. Know that no matter what the circumstances, you can make a choice to regain your power. This simple fact changed my life. As soon as I realized it, I accepted full responsibility for all my *problems*, immediately allowing me to take full responsibility for discovering their *solutions*.

Everything Happens for a Reason

Growing up in England, I had a completely different perspective on how people process problems. In my experience, British people can be incredibly modest and self-deprecating. They are taught to *never* boast or brag, unlike many Americans, and they seldom go on and on about how fantastic everything is. That would be far too expressive. Instead, when you ask a British person how they are doing, they will actually tell you the *truth* and complain about what is currently bothering them at that moment.

When you ask someone in America, "How are you doing?" it's understood to be a rhetorical question; nobody *really* cares about how a person is doing or even waits for their answer. It's simply a greeting. Plus, you will find that in almost all cases, the answer is always the same: "Great!" I am reminded of this stark contrast each time I visit England, where "How are you?" is an invitation for a person to give you a *full* account of how everything is going in their life at that current moment, which may include an in-depth listing of their recent woes.

I did the same thing when I was growing up in England. I loved receiving sympathy; I loved to commiserate, and thus it became a habit to tell anyone who would listen just how bad things were and exactly how miserable I was.

After years of playing the victim, though, a bright and beaming light finally came into my head, and the penny finally dropped. In a nanosecond, I realized that living this way was no longer serving me. I thought about what this way of thinking had brought me. Was I happy living in a place of blame and sorrow? Was it actually enjoyable for me to recount in great detail all the bad things that had happened to me? Did it help me feel any better about my situation? No—in fact, *I was bloody miserable.* So what was I really seeking?

At that moment, I made a firm and conscious decision to live with a different viewpoint. I decided I would begin to accept all the things that happen to me, both the good and the bad, with the same level of *gratitude.* This may sound confusing, but please bear with me. If you can learn to say thank you to your struggles, just as you do to your joys, when challenges cross your path, you will find that in each challenge is a seed of opportunity—an opportunity to grow stronger and more enlightened, to have a deeper sense of who you are, to learn how resilient you have become, and to see setbacks as blessings in disguise.

Although this way of thinking is not always easy, it has been a powerful, transformative tool I've relied on for most of my adult life. It's not that I haven't suffered—I have. And it's not as if I don't acknowledge when life hurts—I'm human, so of course I do. Life has not always been easy for me. I have suffered some things far too painful to write about in the pages of this book, but I decided long ago that those things would never define me and I would choose to believe wholeheartedly that my life was not happening *to me* but rather *for me*, from moment to moment, good or bad.

I have chosen to live my life by this mantra, and I invite you, too, to adopt it as your own personal affirmation: "Everything happens for a reason, and that reason is to benefit me." These words have empowered me through some of the darkest moments in my life. They have helped me always keep my eye on the end result and encouraged me to keep moving forward when things do not turn out the way I wanted them to. Even when I was assaulted, robbed, and experiencing deep loss, my wiser self knew there was a gift there (yes, even there!) and that if I chose to view it this way, I would learn from it and not be the victim of it. This belief has given me great power and courage to persevere.

Spiritual Beings Having a Human Experience

When we perceive the bad things that happen to us to be external, we lose the opportunity to learn from them; they become a fixed part of our lives and experiences that we have no control over. Therefore, we can't grow, we don't learn from them, and we definitely don't learn how to *avoid* repeating them. On the other hand, if we embrace our problems and our adversities as spiritual gifts in our lives, we can discover the lessons they present. In each and every problem we face, there is a seed of opportunity. It's important to remember that we are spiritual beings having a human experience. Because of this, we should try to accept everything that happens in life (the good and the bad) as a spiritual gift.

I realize this may be very difficult to comprehend, especially for anyone who has experienced the mental anguish caused by trauma. Some trauma does not just go away on its own or end by simply ceasing to think about it. It is essential to seek help from a licensed professional if you feel that you are unable to shake your trauma and it is continuing to affect your life in negative ways. Consider a therapist trained in EMDR (eye movement desensitization and reprocessing). EMDR is a form of psychotherapy that enables people to heal from the symptoms and emotional distress that are the result of disturbing life experiences. The results can often be achieved quickly, and healing that once took years of therapy to reach can usually be completed in a matter of weeks with EMDR.[5] If you've experienced severe trauma, it's imperative to seek qualified professional help. Only then can you get on the path to accepting—and growing from—your circumstances, no matter what they are.

It is essential to point out that by accepting these lessons as a part of our human experience, we are not denying that the experience happened or that it may have caused us tremendous pain. Instead, we are accepting that it will *no longer* control our happiness or define who we are. We are simply taking responsibility—and embracing our remarkable ability to respond!

It Can End with Us

Even in cases of terrible pain and shame, the way to transformation is in accepting the situation—not to make it okay but to bring it up to the surface so you can say to it, "You no longer control me or define me."

Take an innocent child who has suffered abuse. They are not in any way responsible for any part of that abuse, or for the pain and shame it has caused them. When the child grows into an adult, they still carry around the pain of that abuse, and for some, it will define their lives and the choices they make. But at some point, as adults, if we can accept how we respond to that painful part of our lives, we can choose how we react to the trauma. We can decide how we will let it enable our spiritual growth or the journeys we take or refuse to take. Perhaps the most beautiful thing is that in acknowledging and bringing our pain to the surface and allowing for wisdom to arise, we can make the decision not to pass on the suffering to our children and grandchildren and to future generations. We can instead accept the *responsibility* to pass on the *wisdom* and the *lessons* we have learned, which is a much richer inheritance.

When Condoleezza Rice, an American diplomat and political scientist who served as the US secretary of state under President George W. Bush, was asked, "How did a young person of color from Birmingham, Alabama, make it all the way to secretary of state?" the first words out of her mouth without hesitation were: "We were never allowed to be victims!"[6] Great leaders are *never* victims. They don't blame others. They know that no matter how grave their circumstances were or how difficult their childhood was, they still have a choice. This empowers them to rise from *victim* to *victor.*

Don't underestimate the power of choice! Choice is one of the most powerful tools we have. When we take control of our lives and fully accept our situation, whatever that may be, we can begin to heal from it and learn from it. It may be something that has dragged you down, knocked you on the floor, down the stairs, and around the block—I get it! I am so sorry that you had to experience it, but *today,* right now, at this very moment, make the decision to no longer let that situation define you.

Suffering Is Optional

Best-selling author and spiritual teacher Byron Katie, whom I have had the pleasure of meeting and studying with, has made it her life's work to educate people on how not to be victims and to take full responsibility for their life's journey. In 1986, Katie had an epiphany: She discovered that when she believed her thoughts, she suffered, but that when she didn't believe them, she didn't suffer.

What Katie discovered is true for every human being. It may sound too simple to believe, but when you really engage with what she calls "The Work," you can truly master your thoughts. The process consists of four simple questions you ask yourself, and the answers to those questions give you the power to turn around your thoughts and feelings. With this simple technique, Katie found a joy within her that has never disappeared, not for a single moment. If you follow the simple rules of her philosophy, you will discover what she teaches: Suffering becomes optional.

Answering the four simple questions, followed by a turnaround process, allows people to analyze their thoughts and choose how to think about the situation they are facing. The method is straightforward and easily accessible for anyone to use, regardless of their background. The four questions to ask yourself are—

1. *Is it true?*
2. *Can I absolutely know that it's true?*
3. *How do I react? What happens when I believe that thought?*
4. *Who would I be without the thought?*

These questions focus on self-inquiry rather than trying to change others or external circumstances. "The Work" encourages individuals to examine their own thoughts and beliefs, taking personal responsibility for their emotions. By questioning negative and painful thoughts, individuals can uncover underlying assumptions and beliefs that cause suffering, leading to profound shifts in perspective.

The process found in her book *Loving What Is* promotes emotional freedom and helps individuals let go of attachments to negative thoughts and emotions, leading to a sense of relief and liberation. "The Work" cultivates awareness and encourages mindfulness and self-study, allowing people to become more present and less reactive to life's challenges. By examining and understanding one's own beliefs, individuals often find greater empathy and compassion for themselves and others, allowing for more meaningful relationships.

The principles are applicable to everyday life and can be used in a wide range of situations, from personal relationships to work-related stress, making it a versatile tool for emotional well-being. The process promotes a nonjudgmental attitude and encourages acceptance of oneself and others, reducing resentment and fostering a more peaceful mindset. By taking responsibility for one's thoughts, individuals often feel more empowered to create change in their lives rather than feeling like victims of circumstance.[7]

After studying with Byron Katie, I passed on her technique to my children. When they had any kind of a problem, I asked them, "What stories are you telling yourself?" I would, of course, allow them to vent, and I would listen to their concerns. But after a while, I would try to get them to see that the problem they were having was tainted by the *stories* they were telling themselves. What they were *believing* about the situation was a great source of the pain they were experiencing. I would try to get them to see that their story, as well as the way they were thinking about it, may not, in fact, be true.

For example, if one of my children came to me and said, "Jane from my class hates me!" or "I have too much homework, and I'll never get it done!" or "Everyone in my class thinks I'm stupid!" I would ask them to challenge that statement with a question: *Is it true?*

Then I asked them: "Can you really and truly *know* that Jane hates you?" or "Do you really believe you will never get your homework done?" or "Does *everyone* in your class think you're stupid?" After some reflecting, their answer was the same: "No, of course not!" The real problem was not the situation itself but what they were *believing* about it. That way of thinking was debilitating and stress-inducing. It was not helpful or empowering in any way.

This type of self-inquiry involves analyzing your thoughts and turning each one around in your mind. When you do this, you usually come to a more balanced and truthful way of seeing a situation: *Jane* does *like me. I have a lot of homework, but I will get it done. Everyone in my class thinks I'm brave because of the questions I ask.* This is just one small example, but you can see that by questioning your beliefs, you will begin to unpack the stories you're telling yourself about the situation. And by doing so, you can eliminate the stress you may be feeling about the story you've created around any given situation or circumstance.

From Victim to Victor

You have the freedom to choose and move forward with a new, more truthful mindset that reflects your wise self, unmarred by false beliefs and painful old stories. You can move from *victim* to *victor*. Here are some key areas where embracing the thought *I will not be a victim—I will be a victor* will help you to flourish:

- **Empowerment:** A victim mentality often places power outside of oneself, leading to feelings of helplessness. By shifting your perspective, you can reclaim your power and feel more in control of your life.

- **Resilience:** Embracing a more empowered mindset fosters resilience. When challenges arise, you'll be more likely to see them as opportunities for growth rather than insurmountable obstacles.
- **Relationships:** A victim mentality can strain relationships. It may lead to negativity or dependency on others for support. Focusing on personal responsibility encourages healthier, more balanced connections.
- **Problem-solving:** Viewing yourself as a victim can hinder critical thinking and problem-solving skills. A proactive approach encourages creativity and resourcefulness in finding solutions.
- **Mental Health:** Continuously identifying as a victim can contribute to anxiety, depression, and other mental health issues. A more empowering outlook can promote emotional well-being.
- **Positive Outlook:** Focusing on what you can change rather than what's been done to you fosters a more optimistic perspective, which can improve overall life satisfaction.
- **Personal Growth:** Recognizing your role in shaping your experiences can lead to significant personal development and a greater sense of fulfillment.

Think of all the things that have previously held you back or prevented you from having the life you want. Now write those things down as a list. This is your list of *limiting beliefs.* Next, take a moment to address each of the items on your list, one at a time, using the worksheet on the next page. On the following page, there is a contract for you to fill out that covers each and every one of your limiting beliefs. Don't get discouraged if your list is long; these limiting emotions took a lifetime to develop, and we are going to spend time breaking them down one by one. Make copies of the following page and use as many pages as needed so that you feel comfortable with each emotion. Then, keep these contract copies to remind yourself of your progress.

Remember, you don't have to be a victim of your circumstances. You can choose how you respond to every situation life throws at you. You can move from victim to victor.

FROM VICTIM TO VICTOR WORKSHEET

I ____________________ (name) choose on this day ____________________ (date) that I will no longer let ______________________________ (experience) define me or prevent me from having the life that I want.

I choose freedom and love, and I forgive myself for choosing to allow ______________________________ to continue to hurt me or hold me back. I release ___________________________ wholly and entirely to God and the Universe.

Signed: ___________________________

(Keep this pledge to yourself in a place where you can remember your progress. Use it to work through each and every limiting belief you hold.)

4

THE TREADMILL OF LIFE

Don't Miss the Magic of the Moment

If it were not for the last minute, I would not get anything done.
—*Rita Mae Brown*

After getting married, both my husband and I were eager to have children. We got lucky, and we had our baby girl after just nine months of marriage, with our baby boy arriving just one year later—our Irish twins. Two years into our marriage, when our children were just toddlers, we decided to buy a piece of land in an area we'd always loved. When we first moved to Atlanta, we would jog in an area called Buckhead, which was located in a beautiful forest in the Paces neighborhood. We had been living in our starter home, a cute little townhouse, with our baby and toddler, but we really wanted an actual house. So when three perfect acres of land popped up for sale in the ideal area, we had what we thought was the brilliant idea of building a 7,000-square-foot custom home.

Never one to shy away from leading new projects, I took over the responsibility of managing the architect, the builder, and the engineers. I'm the type of girl who likes to "grab the bull by the horns," but as a working mother of young children, I already had a lot on my plate. A perennial multitasker and overachiever, I have lived life of to-do lists: business goals, personal projects, home-building tasks, things my kids needed, items for my husband's medical practice that I managed, appointments, meals to plan and groceries to buy, things to shop for—all carefully curated in one large spiral notepad. The busier my life became, the more items were added to my list.

As you may have guessed, I began to feel extremely overwhelmed, and then things really got out of hand. During that time of building our businesses, our home, and our family, I often felt that I was on a fast and unstoppable treadmill. Plus, I had two little ones who were in constant need of my attention.

My day began with the alarm clock going off at 6:30 a.m. I would wake up the kids, struggle to get them both dressed, make a simple breakfast, feed the kids, drink a large cup of coffee, and maybe scarf down a piece of toast before racing out the door to get everyone on the school bus. Often, I would have to drive the children to school because we were running late and they missed the bus. On these mornings, I raced to the car, schlepping my work briefcase, school backpacks, my two kids, and my cell phone. After dropping the children off at school, it was more of the same—speed to work and rush through my day, trying to achieve as much as possible in the limited time I had. Then I would drive home and prepare dinner while my husband picked the kids up from school. My evenings consisted of helping the kids with school projects or reviewing their homework and then getting them ready for bed early enough so I could watch a TV show with my husband and give him some much-needed attention. By the time I finally crawled into bed, I was exhausted. And the following day would be more of the same, day after day, week after week, month after month.

I've always loved spending time with my children, and I wanted to be a hands-on mom in every way possible. However, I also wanted to contribute to our family income and maintain my career. I found that working added to my self-esteem and allowed me to feel productive. Before I got married, I had worked very hard to build a film production company in Aspen, and I wanted to continue to "build my empire," so to speak.

Missing the Magic

I remember one of these insanely busy mornings when my children were in preschool and I was getting them ready for school picture day. The preschool was bringing in a professional photographer to take individual photos of each student, and every parent wanted their child to look their best that day. I picked out my kids' perfect color-coordinated outfits—a beautiful dress for my sweet daughter with a matching bow for her hair, a nice shirt and slacks for my son and a little bow tie. I put everything I needed for work by the front door, along with the kids' backpacks and lunch boxes.

My children at that time were not really into wearing clothes, especially if they didn't like the way the material felt. They would often take what they were wearing off if they didn't care for the outfit or the fabric, preferring to run around in diapers or underwear. Most of the time, I was too exhausted to fight the battle of wills and would give in, allowing them to wear what they wanted. But that morning, I'd finally managed to get them perfectly washed and dressed, and they both looked completely adorable. I, on the other hand, looked like I had been dragged through a hedge backward, with my hair all over the place, no makeup on, and sweat marks running down my once-clean blouse.

I received a phone call from the office with some emergency that needed to be immediately dealt with, so I raced upstairs, trying to multitask by rinsing off and changing my top while speaking on the phone. I didn't plan to leave my little ones alone for long, plus my living room had child safety gates, so the kids were in no danger of escaping. I ended the work call, finished dressing and calmly walked down the stairs, feeling confident that we would make it to school on time and that my kids would (for once) fit in with the other perfectly groomed Southern kids.

And then I was met with the sound of my children giggling. When I opened the safety gate, to my horror I saw my two little angels, their tiny, laughing faces all covered in black marker pen. The time it had taken for me to rinse off and change clothes was precisely all the time my two little ones needed to find a black Sharpie in my bag. My daughter, always the artist, had begun to test out her best artwork on her younger brother's face while he laughed excitedly. In the process of doing this, she had also managed to get black Sharpie all over her dress and hands. My serenity quickly switched to panic, shock, and anger when I realized I would now have to start the entire process *all over again*. I was seething, to say the least.

I scrubbed the kids down, one by one, as I tried to remove Sharpie with Vaseline and makeup remover. When I finally strapped them into their car seats and took a breath, it hit me: In my haste to get them ready and leave on time, I hadn't even thought of taking a moment to snap a picture of their laughing little faces. I hadn't taken the time to capture how cute they looked and how adorable they actually were; I was too late and too stressed to remember to be present in the moment.

We made the fifteen-minute drive to the preschool, and it wasn't until I'd gotten out of the car that I noticed I'd forgotten my shoes. There I was, dressed in a business suit and without shoes, racing into school carrying my son, the backpacks, and lunch bags, holding the hand of my three-year-old daughter as she sauntered behind me. The teachers at the school were very understanding, at least in front of me, but I'm sure they thought I was a crazy lady. On my way to work, I popped into the nearest CVS, bought some flip-flops, and then let the office staff assume I'd just had a pedicure.

That entire experience, while insanely stressful, taught me a *huge* lesson: The only person who judged me that day was ME. Things happen in life, and sometimes it's so much better to just roll with it (as any parent can tell you). The reality of the situation was that I was *still* fully in charge. I could have stopped and taken a moment to laugh and snap a photo. But sometimes, when all you focus on is the stress of the situation, you miss the magic of the moment. If I had taken time to breathe and count to ten before reacting, I would have seen the humor in the situation, and I would have captured for posterity my children's cheeky little faces all covered in Sharpie artwork.

Yes, I was late, and yes, I was stressed. But how much did that preschool photo *really* matter in the scheme of our lives? How much did making it to my work meeting, which could have easily been delayed or rescheduled, matter? As it turned out, those picture-day portraits were not great—they were so bad, in fact, that I never even ordered any prints. That Sharpie moment could have been something we would have laughed at for a lifetime. But that's what happens when you're running on the treadmill of life and you refuse to step off—you miss the joy.

Putting Your Oxygen Mask on First

As I am writing these words, I'm sitting on a plane, waiting for it to take off. The flight attendant just went through the safety presentation, educating the passengers on the best course of action to take in case of an emergency. In addition to all the other emergency procedures, she reminded the passengers to put their own oxygen mask on *first* before helping others. I often think of this as a metaphor, especially in motherhood or in any stressful situation. You have to take care of yourself first so that you can better take care of everyone else later, especially as a mom.

My husband, a trained trauma surgeon, once told me that in emergencies, medical professionals say the first pulse you should take is your own. This means you need to calm yourself down before walking into a triage situation so that you will be levelheaded enough to make the best decisions for the patients you'll encounter. Putting your own oxygen mask on first does not mean you are being selfish; it means you're aware of your own needs so that you can better help and be emotionally available to others.

Self-care is unique for each person. For some, it could be allowing a few moments each day to work on their personal goals. For others, it may be going to bed an hour earlier rather than working late each night. It could even be allowing your kids to eat school lunches instead of spending your precious evenings packing lunch boxes. It can mean doing a little bit *less* for your kids so that you have a little more time for yourself. Unlike many other things in the world, time is precious and finite. We can get more money, we can get more work, we can get more sleep, but we can *never* get more time. Time is the only thing that is truly limited in our lives. None of us know how long we have or when our time will be up. That's why we need to use our time wisely.

If I could go back to the time when I was raising my children—a time when I was extremely harried and stressed—I would stop trying to get so much done and be much more present with them. I would spend more time hugging and cuddling them and less time tidying up knowing, as I do now, that the precious toddler moments pass far too quickly. I now know that in no time at all, they would be off to college, and I would be alone in our home, gazing out the window and listening to the silence, missing the noise, the chatter, and the constant buzz of having little ones around.

Time Is Precious

It wasn't until later in my adult life that I began to treasure the gift of time. As a young woman, I wasted countless hours, days, and even weeks doing things that were a complete waste of my time. I wasted my time with people who didn't fully appreciate me. I wasted time on projects that never came to fruition. I wasted my time as though I had an endless supply of it. I was young and free and extremely unaware of how important time was. So I frequently wasted time in haste to save money—and wasted additional time worrying about not having enough. For example, I'd take the cheapest flight, one with crazy layovers that made travel a nightmare, instead of spending a bit more money to enjoy the journey. Or I would refuse to get medical treatment for a condition, choosing to suffer through it because I thought the cost of care was too high.

After the death of my sister, I realized that all the money in the world, everything I'd worked so hard to save, couldn't give me one more second with her. Not one more moment to tell her how sorry I was or to sit with her and hold her hand. Not one more moment to tell her how much I loved and appreciated her. Not one more moment to tell her I knew she'd felt misunderstood, to express that so many things must have been so difficult for her. No matter how much money I had, I couldn't do any of those things.

To help you understand a little more about the preciousness of time, take out your journal and answer the prompts below.

- *Do I often feel like I don't have enough time in my day?*
- *Do I race through the day, taking care of things, only to discover at the end of the day I didn't feel like I had enough time for anything?*

It is important to periodically assess how you spend your time. What are you prepared to give up to get the life you want? For some people, it will be the hours they spend online, shopping, surfing websites, playing games, excessively checking social media, or trying to keep up with the continuous news cycle. For others, it's a bad health habit or an addiction. For yet others, it may be an unhealthy relationship with a person who does not value their precious time.

Some of us who are parents feel the need to manage each and every aspect of our child's life—homework, activities, sports, even their social calendar. You may feel you need to say yes to everyone's request of your time, which means you're constantly racing from one thing to the next. Trying to be perfect often leads to doing too much, and if you're a parent, it can lead to overparenting, where you feel the need to do everything for your child, so much so that they are slow to learn to self-soothe, overcome boredom, or do simple tasks for themselves.

I was an "overparenter," and it drained so much of my time. I found that I eventually had to give up the need to do everything so perfectly. I had to accept that my kids would not always look their best, that they wouldn't always be dressed in cute and trendy outfits with their hair done perfectly. (Living in the South, there seems to be an unspoken rule that hair should always look fabulous, no matter what.) When I started allowing my little ones to choose their own outfits and dress themselves, they sometimes looked ridiculous, and their hair didn't resemble any kind of style, but everyone survived. I also started cooking a lot less. We ate prepared food or takeout a couple of nights a week, and we were just fine. I also decided I no longer needed to attend every board meeting, every PTA meeting, every book club. I began to say no . . . no . . . NO!

Swapping To-Do for To-Be

Saying no can be freeing. When you begin to say no to things, it helps you become aware of the things you actually want to say yes to. It frees up space for the most important things in your life. Try putting down your to-do list and instead creating a *to-be* list. Be present as you envision who you'd like to be and what you'd be doing if you had the time to do it. Go inward and ask yourself, *What am I sensing? What am I seeing? What am I hearing?*

If you allow yourself to be fully present in the current moment, you'll realize that in many instances, stress is an illusion. It's created from memories of the past or fear of the future—and in those cases, it's not real. Ask yourself these questions:

- *What do I want to be?*
- *How do I want my life to look?*
- *What are my goals?*
- *How do I want to spend my precious time?*
- *What will I be today before I write my to-do list? Will I be happy? Will I be healthy? Will I be calm?*
- *Will I choose to be present with my children, my friends, and my loved ones?*
- *Will I make time for the people and things that are truly important to me and my well-being?*
- *What will I do to incorporate a healthier attitude into my daily living—in mind, body, and spirit?*

As you reflect on your answers to these questions, make sure *you* are first on your to-do list. In order to care for others, you must first attend to your own self-care and make it a priority each day to practice mindfulness.

Taking Your Time Back

How you start your day can determine how you live your life. I recommend beginning each day on a positive note, even if this means getting up a little bit before everyone else. For some people, this can be starting their day on their knees and thanking God for every blessing in your life. For some, it may be taking a relaxing shower or having a time of quiet meditation. Think about what you need to do to be spiritually centered and present. Then do those things *first*—before you do anything else.

Maybe your current daily schedule doesn't allow you to take much time in the morning for yourself. Set your alarm for fifteen minutes earlier, so you can give yourself just a little bit of me time. Put the most important things on your schedule, such as a workout like a walk or a run. (I strongly recommend adding exercise to your routine.)

For me, it's yoga. This practice has helped me recover from chronic back and neck pain after a terrible skiing accident. Yoga allows me to remain strong and flexible while helping me clear my mind and stay focused. If I find myself sitting for too long at the computer while working or writing, I make sure I do extra stretches for my back and neck. Swimming is another great exercise for many people, because your body is supported by the water. Exercise can be anything you enjoy. Determine what works best for you, and then make time to do it. If you cannot do it at the beginning of your day, then put it on your calendar as one of your appointments for the day. Or partner with a friend and be exercise buddies who hold each other accountable. No matter what you choose, do what works best for *you*.

I get it. Sometimes, it's hard to just get through the day. At those times, make a decision to do the next *right* thing! This is not a strategic game of chess, so there's no need to overthink it. We can't always be perfect, but commit to doing something positive in the direction of your goals. Breathe and be kind to yourself. You've got this!

SIMPLE STRATEGIES FOR BEING AT YOUR BEST

- Start your day with an organized plan of things that are important to you—things that you want to achieve.
- Put yourself at the top of your plan, so you can achieve your tasks, work, and goals in an organized and mindful way.
- Don't allow stress to rule your day. Breathe through stress, so that you can address things more calmly and easily.
- Remember, you are the architect of your life and your schedule, you are in control of your day and your time; find a way for it *not* to control you.

5

MIND OVER MATTER

Mental Strength Is a Powerful Tool—Train It and Use It Well

Success does not always go to the
man with the master plan, but
sooner or later, the one who wins
is the one who thinks he can.
—*Unknown*

When you are working toward a particular goal, whatever that goal may be, you must believe in yourself—and in your true potential—without a shadow of a doubt. If you lose faith in yourself, all is lost. I think this journey began for me when I turned twenty-one and read the book *The Power of Your Subconscious Mind* by Joseph Murphy. Although this was an old bestseller, the philosophy presented in it changed my life.

Up until that point, I don't believe I had truly understood my full potential. By that I mean, I did not understand or believe that I had any power over my mind or my thoughts. I simply assumed my thoughts came and went in a jumbled fashion, and I often spoke ill of myself or berated myself for not being perfect. Murphy's book became like my Bible, and I functioned as a Jedi Knight, following all of the suggestions, which shaped my mind into a powerful tool that was able to manifest my destiny. You may think this sounds insane, but let me guide you back to the opening quote from this chapter: "Success does not always go to the man with the master plan, but sooner or later, the one who wins is the one who thinks he can." This has not only been true for me but for millions of people around the world. Basically, if you believe you are going to fail at something, you probably will.

My husband worked as an orthopedic surgeon for over thirty years, and he would often tell me he knew which patients he operated on were going to have the most success, even just after meeting them at the pre-op. Besides not smoking, not drinking excessively, and having other healthy habits, the patient's attitude accounted for much of their successful outcome. Patients who were depressed or lacked the ability to think positively about the experience would often have a more difficult recovery than those who were positive and cheerful about the outcome of their surgery.

Finding Your Why

It is no secret that the most successful people in life are the ones who believe in themselves. They may have had to work hard and dedicate themselves to their craft, but along the way, they never gave up on their dreams. Others may have criticized their aspirations or told them it could never work, but they believed, they persisted, and they continued on until they were successful. For many of us, this is very difficult to do. We let self-doubt and self-criticism seep in, or we allow the viewpoints of others to rule our daily lives.

How many of your goals have you quashed because somebody else told you they were impossible? Or because you were too afraid to say them out loud? Or because you convinced yourself they were out of reach? The words may have come from a well-meaning parent, family member, friend, or someone else who was trying to "protect" you from failure or disappointment based on their own limited way of thinking. Or it might have been your own false beliefs about your capabilities that held you back.

Take out your journal and ask yourself these questions, then write down the answers:

- *What is my vision for my magnificent life?*
- *What is the one thing I really want to achieve in this life, and why do I want to achieve it?*
- *What do I want to be remembered for?*
- *What will my legacy be?*

For some people, the goal is to make money, and that is fine, but think a little deeper here. *Why* do you want to make money? Is it because you want to have nice things, buy a house, and start a family, or do you see money as simply having power? Some individuals want to travel the world with their money. Do you want to see new places and have new experiences, or do you just want to say that you have been to a particular country? What exactly is it that you want?

It is essential to be very clear about *why* you want to achieve a specific goal. Otherwise, some of the goals you work so hard to attain won't be very rewarding once you accomplish them. You have to really examine the *why* of your goals and figure out what the driving force is behind them in order to achieve them—and then be happy with the results.

Manifest It

It's easy to set a low bar for ourselves, afraid of aiming too high in order to protect ourselves from failure. But don't sell yourself short. Aiming too low is the failure, as you will end up exactly where you set out to go. If you believe (as I do) that we all play a part in manifesting our destiny, then you will always aim high.

When I was a little girl growing up in Yorkshire, England, I always dreamt big. I had this feeling that my life would be *magnificent*. I would sit for hours day-dreaming about my future as I played with my dolls or played in the backstreets. I would imagine all the things I would buy when I had lots of money—all the great things I would do for myself and my brothers and sisters. I would name each sibling and think of what I could purchase for them when I became rich. I worked my way down my list from the oldest to the youngest, carefully calculating how much money I would need to buy them a car, a house, a cool motorbike, or fancy clothes. While it may seem materialistic for a child that young to be thinking about money so much, I now realize that childhood goal was more about being able to help my family; it was a generous and loving in intention. By the time I got to my own needs on my imaginary list, the goal was only one thing, like the latest toy or doll. Meanwhile, I'd spent most of my time imagining giving my siblings much more extravagant gifts.

Later, after I moved to America and after years of hard work and sheer determination, I was on my way to the magnificent life I'd imagined as a child. I had a beautiful home that I'd filled with fine furniture, artwork, and luxury décor. Eventually, my parents came to visit from England. After I gave them a tour of our home, my sweet and saintly mother stared out a window, admiring the elegant grounds, the pool and spa, the outdoor living area, the beautifully landscaped gardens, and the many trees we'd planted on the three-acre property. Then she turned to me and said, "Who would have imagined you would end up with all of this?" My mother didn't have a mean bone in her body, so she meant this with the *best* intentions.

My first reaction to her comment was one of complete shock, because I always knew I would end up having a magnificent life, so I simply responded with a smile: "Me, mum—*I* imagined it."

I am a huge believer in manifestation. The language of manifestation goes back to before biblical times. If you have read the Bible, you will see it contains many manifestation quotes:

"Ask, and it shall be given to you."

"Seek, and you will find."

"Knock, and the door will be opened to you."

"As you sow, so shall you reap."

"Keep your heart with all vigilance, for from it flow thc springs of life."

With manifestation, you have to get to the point where you know, without a shadow of a doubt, that you will have the life you want and deserve. You possess both the power of thought and the power of will. Each one of us can use these divine gifts to our advantage, not just for personal gain but for divine goodness. I believe we are here to spread love and light, to manifest our way on this incredible spiritual journey. Manifestation is a tool, and like all spiritual tools, you have to work with it for it to be effective. For most of my adult life, I have written down my goals and my manifestations. Sometimes when I come across those tattered, handwritten pages, I gaze at the sentences I once wrote, in awe of how many of my manifestations actually came true.

I recently partnered with a wonderful spiritual app called Khuda. This app will personalize your goals and help you manifest them. Khuda basically functions as a spiritual companion, offering insight, comfort, and guidance inspired by timeless spiritual teachings. It's designed to help users find clarity, purpose, and connection to their inner wisdom, and it easily allows for personal manifestations. I wish this app had been available when I began my spiritual journey. I've spent countless hours journaling and writing page after page of my personal mantras and manifestations, and now you can do it through an app.

Manly P. Hall was a Canadian author, lecturer, astrologer, and spiritual guru who spent his seventy-year career giving thousands of lectures and publishing over 150 monographs. The best-known is *The Secret Teachings of All Ages,* which he published in 1928. In 1934, he founded the Philosophical Research Society in Los Angeles. Hall believed that true spirituality was a mental attitude: "It is the outlook of the mind that has freed itself from prejudice, materialism, and fear, and the great work of the initiate is to spread the light. Not only to spread the light but to be the light." Manifesting the life we want begins with our thoughts, and the quality of our thoughts and how they are managed is the foundation of our well-being.

Make a Plan

Take a moment right now to think about the life you have imagined for yourself. I'm not talking about posting your wildest dreams on Pinterest or haphazardly creating a vision board with images of fancy cars or extravagant homes torn out of magazines, with no actionable plan on how to get those things. I'm talking about doing what you know you are capable of achieving in this life. This may sound impossible, especially if right now your goal seems too far out of reach or you're not clear on it yet and it's just a tiny glimmer in your imagination. Still, allow yourself some dedicated quiet time to dream and take it one step at a time.

It's easy for us to spend a lifetime letting negative thoughts talk us out of living, even from taking that first baby step. But remember, negative thoughts attract negativity. Don't give these thoughts any power. Speak highly and kindly of yourself and seek out the good in others. Don't allow doubt to cripple your beliefs. This is a step in the right direction. Be conscious of the possibility of change—and welcome it. Give your personal best and expect the best in others. Forget the past—it doesn't equal your future. Stop making excuses for yourself and your imagined limits. Put one foot in front of the other, dust off the cobwebs, wipe away the tears, and get serious about your goals. Don't just think it—know it, feel it, believe it!

Have an actionable plan and work on it daily until you achieve your dreams. Take a moment to write down your goals in your journal. The devil is in the details.

PUTTING YOUR GOALS DOWN ON PAPER

What do you want to achieve today? #goals

This week:

This year:

Five years:

Ten years:

Lifetime:

I think you get the idea. Racehorses wear blinders so they can keep their vision directed forward and not get distracted by the things around them; their focus is solely on the path ahead. This is how we need to be about our goals, focused on our own journey and finish line.

People with a positive mental attitude seem to be healthier, happier people, living lives of richness and contentment. According to Harvard Health Publishing, a person's mental state has a pronounced effect on their overall physical health. Multiple studies have clearly shown that mindfulness reduces the risk of stress-related illnesses such as heart disease.[8] So make that the plan, take that first step toward achieving your dream, and welcome the possibility of change.

Happiness Is the Way

In one of my yoga classes, a giant sign on the wall reads: "There is no way to happiness—happiness is the way." It took me a moment to understand what this really means. Ultimately, if you want happiness, be happy! This may sound ridiculous, but it's actually a very powerful message. Positive thoughts have a magnetic attraction the same way as negative thoughts; they attract more positive thoughts. It's the same with positive actions, positive people, and positive experiences.

Living a happy life is about *being* from moment to moment. Sometimes, you may need to have the attitude of "Fake it till you make it." Yes, that's right—do as happy people do. What do you notice about the happy people in your life? Observe what they do—and then try to emulate it. I've practiced "Fake it till you make it" to help me get through various stages of my life when happiness or mindfulness were not second nature. There were times when it was difficult to just get through the day, so on those days, I employed various tricks to force myself to feel better about whatever it was I needed to do. Below are some practices that have helped me—practices that science has shown are effective—to get into and *maintain* a positive state of being—without being a victim of toxic positivity.

Physical Exercise

Many independent scientific studies have confirmed the link between physical exercise and improved mental health. Exercise increases blood flow and endorphins that allow us to feel good about ourselves. If you are feeling "down in the dumps," the first thing to try is to get some exercise. Every time my doctor husband reminds me of this during my periods of sadness, I often want to hiss at him or punch him in the face. But instead, I bite my tongue and put on my running shoes.

Initially, the first half mile of my run-walk involves going through a long mental list of how much I suck at running and lamenting my current lack of physical conditioning, followed by going through a long mental list of how I don't run enough, exercise enough, lift weights enough, do yoga enough, etc. Basically, a whole storm of negative thoughts. But then, almost out of nowhere, my attitude swiftly changes. I notice a beautiful tree or a pretty landscape, or perhaps I see a wildflower or a person walking a cute little dog. I hear the sounds of nature. My breathing becomes less frantic, and I begin to feel a lot better. And then I *exorcise* whatever had been previously holding me back. I have learned that *exercise* can *exorcise* my negativity, and it always works. Sometimes, it takes a little longer, and I have to do something a little more strenuous, like a challenging hike. But whenever I exercise, I find that after I'm done, my thoughts feel a whole lot lighter than they were before I started.

Yoga

Yoga has been a lifesaver for me. This is not just because of the stretching and strengthening it has on my body, but also because it combines the mind, body, and spirit. Yoga has been a phenomenal addition to my life, and I believe I have been able to achieve great things as a result of my decades-long practice.

I've been practicing yoga ever since a terrible ski accident I had in my twenties, which damaged my back and neck. One day, during my wilder life as a daredevil skier, I had an unfortunate accident on a double black diamond run on Aspen Mountain. I hit a rock and flew off a cliff, unable to catch my balance on the catwalk in time. I flew through the air until I hit a pine tree, then fell off the side of the cliff, ultimately into a long, remote ravine. I was lucky to be found by the Aspen Ski Patrol employees, who worked diligently to locate me just before hypothermia set in. I sustained a couple of broken ribs and a severe cervical sprain, but thanks to their incredible rescue operation, I am still on this earth—and my gratitude for them is immeasurable.

Yoga was vital and instrumental in my recovery process, helping me regain strength and flexibility after the accident. If you've never done yoga before, think of it as a personal journey with your own body. And if you're reading this and telling yourself, *Oh, I could never do yoga!* be encouraged. *Everyone* can do yoga—no matter what their physical condition is when they start.

A couple of years ago, I had the honor of taking a class with the venerable yoga instructor Tao Porchon-Lynch. I met Tao when she was ninety-nine years old, and she'd come to the Lead with Love event in Aspen to teach a yoga class to the hundreds of attendees. In a word, she was *magnificent.* Despite the low oxygen, due to being nine thousand feet above sea level, Tao appeared fitter than most of the other students in the class, effortlessly moving through the various poses. I watched her push her palms into the mat as she gracefully lifted her body into a *Tolasana*, a difficult pose where you sit with your legs crossed in the lotus pose and then use the strength of your core, shoulders, and arms to lift yourself up. I still can't do the Tolasana pose, but Tao did it with such ease and grace that the entire class gasped in amazement at her abilities. I later had the pleasure of speaking with her privately. During our conversation, I looked down at her feet, noticing her beautiful red toenail polish. She told me that she'd been painting her toenails that way since she was in her early twenties and that the beautiful red polish now reminded her that she was still young.

Tao exuded joy in every aspect of her being. The people who met her would feel this joy when they were around her, and you could bask in the light that shone from her spirit. She told me that yoga is a personal experience you have with your own body, so you meet it where you are and work with it to the best of your abilities. A few years back, Tao needed a hip replacement, and she often had aches and pains, but she never let it prevent her from doing yoga. She would just meet it where she was and keep working at it. *If she can be so joyous, so serene, after having a hip replaced,* I told myself, *then all of us can.* Tao was the epitome of *mind over matter*. After my inspiring conversation with her, I made a silent pledge to be more like Tao and to make it my life's goal to exude joy like she did.

Spirituality Practices

An article on spirituality and mental health in *TIME* magazine outlined how, just like is the case with those who exercise, people who have some form of spiritual belief tend to be happier than those who don't. Those who believe in a higher power, or a power greater than themselves, have a belief system to turn to when things collapse or life gets extremely tough. Finding a greater sense of purpose or belief in something bigger than yourself is what often pulls individuals through difficult situations.[9]

For my incredible mother, it was her religion. She was a devout Catholic, a quietly religious person who lived a good and honest life and tried to live by the teachings of Jesus. She was loving and nonjudgmental; she gave most of her things away and worked directly with people who were sick and suffering. In short, she was an incredibly kind and humble person who never spoke a bad word about anyone; she was always able to see the good in people. She would often tell me that her faith had helped her survive the death of three of her children: my sister Jackie, who was twenty-nine when she passed away, a two-year-old daughter, who died before I was born, and a stillborn son, who she delivered at six-months gestation. Mum suffered much more than any mother should ever suffer, mourning the death of three of her children, but she still was able to see the good in the world. Her faith helped her believe that her children were with God, and she found peace in that.

Faith can help you overcome the bad times, guide you to a higher purpose, and allow you to believe in something bigger than this world. Because faith is so unique for everyone, I am not one to judge a person for what they believe. We are all the same under the eyes of God and the Universe. When you believe in something greater than yourself and find your group of people, or as I like to call it, your tribe, there is no filter needed, no worries about being judged—you just understand each other.

Although I was raised Catholic, I found that many of the people I met during my time attending church were not living in the way of Jesus. It greatly disturbed me. I witnessed church members who were unkind to or unaccepting of others. This contrasted with the teachings of Jesus, which are beautiful and pure. His message was to selflessly *love* others: Love your enemies as yourself. Turn the other cheek and forgive. Serve one another. Don't steal. Don't kill. Don't judge. Jesus helped the sick, the poor, and the destitute. His life was not about power or wealth but about forgiveness, about leading by example and being of service.

Just think about this for a moment: If we could all follow these teachings, there would be no wars, no murders, no robberies, no gun violence, no school shootings. There would be no hatred against the people who do not see the world the same way we see it. Politicians would not talk about "us versus them." We would have more peace. We would not judge people under a lens that we created. Try to imagine that world for a moment.

Self-Love

Have you ever listened to the words and phrases you tell yourself? What do you keep saying to yourself, over and over again? In my teenage years, I often spoke down to myself. To address this negative thinking, I began working with a therapist when I was twenty-five. Early on, she asked me this simple question: "What are some of the thoughts in your head about yourself, and how do you speak to yourself?"

Think about a typical day as you prepare for work, do your job or attend school, or go about your day-to-day activities. What thoughts are you telling yourself? My therapist made me realize that I often said really mean things to myself and I lacked self-compassion. For example, while I was getting ready for work in the morning, I would say to myself, *You look ridiculous in that outfit.* I would call myself *stupid* if I were running late. I would think, *Don't be such an idiot*, after asking a question during my morning conference call or meeting. I often told myself I had ruined something or made it worse by opening my mouth. And with my therapist's help, I realized this was a lot of negative self-talk.

My therapist asked me to do a simple task to become aware of the negative messages I was telling myself. She asked me to spend a day noticing my self-talk and observing my thoughts. Then, she asked me to find a heavy book, pick it up, and carry it around with me all day. At the precise moment when I became aware of any negative thought, she told me to drop the book hard on the ground so it would make a loud noise. As the book hit the ground with a bang, she told me to say out loud, "STOP!"

The first day I did this exercise, I dropped the book at least a hundred times, but it did the trick of alerting me to my negative mindset and seeing my self-deprecating comments in a new light. (If you choose to do this, you may want to do it when you're home alone so you don't look like a complete nutcase dropping heavy books all the time!) Trust me, this exercise works. By day three, I had dropped the book only twice. I only had to do it for four days before banishing my damaging self-talk. After doing that simple but highly effective exercise, I have never talked negatively to myself.

Another way to stop negative self-talk is to wear an elastic band around one of your wrists. Snap it so it pings you whenever you engage in negative self-talk. This can be very effective, and it's easy to do in public without people noticing. Snap that band every time you think a negative thought about yourself or pick on yourself.

Be conscious of how you select your thoughts each day. Just as you may choose healthy meals or ways of living, choose healthy thoughts each and every day. Try to harvest self-compassion and kindness in the way you speak to yourself, and talk to yourself as though you're talking to a friend—and then be your own best friend.

Be Present

Spending time in the present moment is an effective way to avoid being paralyzed by worry and fear. That's because when we choose to live in the present, we are no longer dwelling on the past or fearing the future.

There is an old Samurai legend outlined in *Journey to Center* by Thomas Crum, whose teachings I greatly admire. It goes like this: A man is being chased through a field by a wild and ferocious bear. As he races quickly away from the bears's ravaging claws, he finds himself at the edge of a cliff. As he looks down to jump off the cliff, he notices a lion circling below, so he dangles below the cliff's precipice, holding only a vine. As the man dangles over the cliff, caught between the bear's claws above and the lion circling below, he has no idea what to do. Either way leads to imminent death. Then a tiny mouse appears and begins to chew on the vine. At that precise moment, the man notices a plump, wild strawberry right in front of him. He picks the delicious strawberry with his free hand and pops it into his mouth.[10] This wise, ancient, and beautiful story highlights how often, amid our problems and challenges, we miss life's best moments. The bear above could represent the past, and the lion below could represent the future. Too often, we find ourselves living between the past or the future and not enjoying the present moment, the moment when the delicious wild strawberry is right in front of us.

Letting Go of Fear

We are living in the era of a constantly breaking news cycle. We are assaulted daily, minute by minute and hour by hour, with everything that is happening in the world. Social media bombards us with stories that are sensational and enticing but also fear-producing. We understand that the headlines are designed for clicks, and the more viewers a channel has, the more they can charge for the advertising that appears on their site. It is a highly successful business, and it's easy to get caught up in the drama of it all.

Although having easy access to news means that we have the ability to be well-informed about local and world events, we're also inundated with terrible and tragic stories of death, fear, and suffering. It's no wonder so many adults and children are anxious and depressed today. Not to mention, so many news networks rake in millions of dollars by fearmongering with pieces created to spread fear and anxiety. It seems that every time I tune in, I learn about yet another thing to be afraid of.

While it's good to be informed, it is also important that we don't allow our lives to be ruled by fear. Fear is crippling, and I am not buying or giving in to it. I refuse to give in to fear. I like to think of the acronym for *FEAR* as Fake Evidence Appearing Real. That simple phrase alone has helped me conquer some of my greatest fears, allowing me to paraglide even though I had a fear of heights, scuba dive even though I had a fear of water. Conquering fear has allowed me to travel the world, open new businesses, and ski double black diamond, mogul-covered runs.

Now, this isn't about totally getting rid of fear, because everyone experiences those feelings, and some fears are reasonable if they can help guide us away from unsafe situations. It's helpful to think of fear as a gift that allows us to avoid dangerous or life-threatening conditions. Fear can warn us of impending danger and enable us to take action to prevent injury or death. But take a moment to ask yourself if what you're afraid of is valid or just imagined fear. Think about all the things you've worried about in your life. Then ask yourself the following questions: *How many of my greatest fears ever materialized? How many years have I spent worrying about something that may never happen? Why am I choosing to give fear this power over myself?*

I never feared being held up in an armed robbery, yet I wasted years worrying about so many other things that never actually happened. That makes me laugh a little. Here I am writing a self-help book revealing how I overcame something so terrifying, and yet it was never one of my fears. This goes to show what a complete waste of time living in fear is. Choose today not to allow fear to control your life, and you will live a life with much more peace, joy, and potential.

I have benefited profoundly from the teachings of Deepak Chopra, especially his book *The Seven Spiritual Laws of Success*, which I have used as my spiritual guide for many years. One of Chopra's most powerful teachings from that book (in my opinion) is what he calls the Law of Detachment. He writes: "In detachment lies the wisdom of uncertainty . . . In the wisdom of uncertainty lies the freedom from our past, from the known, which is the prison of past conditioning. In our willingness to step into the unknown, the field of all possibilities, we surrender ourselves to the creative mind that orchestrates the dance of the universe."[11] During the stressful and trying times in my life, I have used this universal Law of Detachment to help me surrender to the outcome of difficult circumstances.

Allowing Change

Clutching tightly to a person or set of circumstances or forcing one's will on a situation eliminates the possibility of change happening naturally. The more you try to force change, the less likelihood there is of things *actually* changing. Trying to control everything prevents the Universe from working its magic. Control is an illusion; when we try to control someone or something, paradoxically *we are controlled* by the person or situation. It doesn't matter if we are right or think we need to prove our point to the other person. It simply doesn't matter. You have to be able to let it go for change to happen. People will resist our attempts to change them or double down on their efforts not to change, but when we detach and surrender, that's when things can truly change.

One of my favorite quotes comes from internationally renowned author and motivational speaker Dr. Wayne Dyer. It's a quote my children are so tired of hearing that they will often humorously quote it back to me when I am facing a challenge: "When you change the way you look at things, the things you look at change." In Dr. Dyer's book *The Power of Gratitude: Live Each Day Mindful of Your Blessings*, it is the central idea to his teachings on how our perception can shape our reality. When we allow ourselves to see things from a different point of view, the situation we are faced with will often change. Our beliefs, perceptions, and attitudes have a profound effect on how we interpret a situation and interact with it. If we shift our mindset or outlook on a particular situation, person, or problem, what we see or experience can also transform. If you allow yourself to approach a challenging situation with a positive or open mind, you will find opportunities or lessons that you wouldn't have noticed before. Not only does our mindset change, but our life changes around us.

Remember that whatever you think about will directly impact the outcome of your life and your experiences. If you're feeling discouraged about something in your life, remember the advice to "fake it till you make it"—and then do that until you actually begin to feel better. Start by smiling and focusing only on the things that bring you joy. This will help you change your mindset and improve your overall mood. Find your tribe, your group, anyone who you find supportive. Commit to a belief system. Look for meaning in life and events. Get out of your comfort zone and do something you haven't done before. Focus on the present moment and try to forget about your past or future worries. Pay attention to what makes you happy by living one day at a time or even one hour at a time. Be present and find joy *in this moment.*

I have come up with some of my own beliefs that have guided me in training my mind toward a life of more joy, and I want to share them with you. I invite you to adopt any of these beliefs as affirmations and incorporate them into your own journey in any way that is helpful. You can write them down on sticky notes and put them on your bathroom mirror or whisper them softly to yourself when you're feeling down or whatever else works for you. Remember, there is no wrong way when you're stepping in the direction of joy.

- I believe in the best outcome of all my situations.
- I believe in myself and my abilities.
- I believe in my future and in new beginnings.
- I believe that the Universe will reward me for my excellent work.
- I believe in life's magic.
- I believe in miracles.
- I believe there is a way it *can* be done.
- I believe I will meet the right people to help me along the way.
- I believe in the goodness of all people.
- I believe I *can* make a difference.

- I believe that today I will begin the best part of my life.
- I believe that I am good enough for greatness and that all good things will come my way.

When you choose success over failure, the present gifts over past or future worries, and a life of joy and self-confidence over a life of negativity and self-doubt, you will reach—and surpass—your goals. You'll accomplish even more than you ever dreamed possible, and remember—it all begins with welcoming positive change into your life.

6

THE POWER OF GRATITUDE

Live Each Day Mindful of Your Blessings

Be thankful for what you have;
you'll have more. If you concentrate
on what you don't have, you will
never, ever have enough.
—*Oprah Winfrey*

One of the main reasons I chose to write this book was to share the joy I have found from my gratitude practice. Gratitude has helped me get through some of life's most challenging moments. Gratitude is the most important and fascinating mental tool we have to alleviate problems or brighten our outlook on life. The word *gratitude* comes from the Latin word *gratus*, which means "pleasing" or "thankful." Gratitude at its most basic form can be the feeling of appreciation we have for the kindness of others, the beauty they add to our lives, the help they provide, the kind words they say to us, or the favors they do for us. Gratitude can also be a feeling of deep thankfulness—thankfulness for all the good things in life, including the simple things like having a place to live, food to eat, clean water to drink, friends and family, and good health. Gratitude is a feeling that comes from within, and it's something that cannot be taken from us.

According to *Psychology Today*, "Functional brain MRIs of people assigned a task that stimulates the expression of gratitude, show lasting changes in the prefrontal cortex that heighten sensitivity to future experiences of gratitude." Basically, feeling grateful teaches your brain to feel grateful in the future. It functions almost like a muscle—the more you train it, the stronger it becomes.

The same article in *Psychology Today* explains that over time, feeling grateful boosts happiness and fosters both physical and psychological health, even among those struggling with mental health issues. Studies show that practicing gratitude curbs the use of words expressing negative emotions and shifts inner attention away from such negative emotions as resentment and envy, minimizing the possibility of ruminating, which is a hallmark of depression. Scientists who have studied gratitude have found it has been shown to improve mental health, decrease anxiety and depression, increase physical health and emotional resilience, allow for greater empathy and compassion, improve self-esteem, and result in better sleep. Most of all, gratitude increases feelings of happiness.[12]

It is not always easy to be grateful, especially when life is challenging or we are suffering mentally or physically. However, like most new endeavors, if we start with small exercises in gratitude, it becomes easier to practice. Anyone who has given birth to a child will understand this feeling of gratitude. I remember the moment after delivering each of my children, when I was discharged from the hospital and ready to bring our baby home. As we headed out (after my husband finally managed to install the infant car seat), with that little bundle of joy safely buckled in behind me, an overwhelming feeling of *gratitude* came over me. I wept as I remembered the last nine months of trying to do everything right to give my baby the best possible start in life, and the realization of my hard work paying off. Holding my child was the best feeling in the world, and the gratitude I felt in that one moment was simply overwhelming.

You may have experienced a similar feeling of gratitude when you completed a major project, passed an exam or a driving test, done well at school or at work, baked a delicious cake, picked a bouquet of beautiful flowers you grew in your garden, received a nice note or card from a friend or coworker, or even just tidied up your house and made it cozy. Gratitude is a magical feeling, and the more you practice and recognize it, the more it will appear in your life.

Practicing Gratitude

Andy Stanley, an American author, speaker, and pastor who is the founder of North Point Ministries in Atlanta, Georgia, explained in one of his better-known sermons that unexpressed gratitude is experienced by the other person as ingratitude. It is the *expression* of gratitude that is needed for the other person to know that we are grateful. To be grateful requires humility. Unexpressed gratitude can mean that we have an inflated view of ourselves and our accomplishments. (Arrogant people are usually the most ungrateful people.)

For some people, expressing gratitude out loud may feel vulnerable, but in reality it is a sign of strength. Some of our most outstanding achievements, if we take a realistic look at them, often involve somebody helping us along the way. Stanley expressed the necessity of thanking the people who have helped us and worked with us—whether it be a parent, family member, spouse, coworker, or friend—and taking the time to acknowledge them.[13] Ask yourself, *If I haven't expressed gratitude to that person, why not?*

Being Grateful in Tough Times

Ironically, when I was writing this chapter on gratitude, it came at one of the most challenging times in my life. My beautiful, loving mother was dying, and she was in the final days of her life in a hospice facility. I was devastated and finding it extremely difficult to find *any* gratitude in the situation. I loved Mum with all of my heart, and I will mourn her for the rest of my days. I miss our laughter-filled conversations with me filling her in on what my kids were doing and her expressing how happy she was for us. I miss hearing her sweet voice, her kind eyes, and her beautiful smile. It was almost impossible to say goodbye to her and to watch her decline as she drifted ever so slowly away to the angels.

At that time, I had just lost my dear friend Alicia, who passed away from a terminal lung condition. Alicia's daughter and I had spent a painful ten days in the ICU watching her die, praying together, crying together, and mourning the loss of both of our mothers. It was almost as if the Universe wanted to fully make sure I knew what I was talking about before I wrote about gratitude. There may not seem to be an obvious link between the grief of losing someone and gratitude, but there is. When you have lost a loved one, you suffer, but you also slowly begin to appreciate everything so much more. When you no longer take life for granted, you discover true gratitude. You realize that even on our darkest days, there is always something to be grateful for.

I am aware that there are people who have suffered a lot more than I have, and yet they still find gratitude each day. A friend of mine tragically lost her daughter to an accidental fentanyl overdose shortly after her daughter's high school graduation. The tragedy struck right after my friend had successfully overcome a rare type of non-Hodgkin's lymphoma. The loss of a child is something no parent should ever have to endure, and my friend's pain was raw and palpable. Yet, as part of her healing journey, she takes the time to write and post on social media the most magnificent reflections. I found a gravitational pull drawing me to her posts, perhaps because they reminded me of losing my sister. Her words comforted my soul. I know that my friend's writing is cathartic and gives her space to mourn and navigate this unimaginable loss, but it also gives space to anyone else who has lost someone. Her writing has one common theme: *gratitude*. She finds gratitude in her daily life, in her art, with her friends, in nature, and in the love she has for her family. She navigates grief but is guided by gratitude. I find this both magnificent and incredibly inspiring.

The pain of losing a loved one, or the death of a loving relationship, obviously hurts, and it takes time to heal and for your heart to recover. But if you sit each day in gratitude and spend a few moments feeling the love you have for them—not the loss—you will find comfort in the knowledge that *you* have that love in your heart. You have had a beautiful experience with another human being who allowed you to feel this love, and *there is gratitude in that.*

I have many friends who have walked the path to sobriety tell me that they count gratitude as one of the single most important foundations of their recovery. Gratitude is what keeps them sober each and every day. At the Hazelden Betty Ford Clinic, and in many other rehabilitation programs, gratitude is taught as a central pillar for early addiction recovery. It has helped many addicts get clean and sober and stay that way for many years.[14]

A now sober friend of mine told me a story explaining how gratitude had saved him. Before he got sober, he was living a miserable life. Most people saw him as a person who had everything—all the luck in the world—but he still was unhappy. Early in his sobriety, he shared with his sponsor that he was still struggling and still sad. From an outsider's perspective, my friend had everything, but he was still miserable. His sponsor then asked him to think of what he had in life to be grateful for. My friend paused for a moment, then realized he was drawing a blank. During the pause in his thinking, the sponsor asked him, "Do you have a place to sleep tonight?"

"Yes," he answered in surprise, as he hadn't thought of this.

"Do you have food in your refrigerator at home?" the sponsor continued.

"Why, of course, yes," my friend answered.

"Do you have gas in your car?"

"Yes," my friend said slowly, beginning to realize where his sponsor was going with this.

"And are you in reasonable health?"

My friend then smiled as he realized he, in fact, had a lot to be grateful for. He said that those types of self-reflections have gotten him through some tough times.

Gratitude isn't about ignoring life's difficulties but rather about maintaining a balanced perspective. It teaches us to savor the good, even when life is tough. Over time, gratitude can turn into a guiding force, helping us maintain a sense of fulfillment and contentment regardless of external circumstances.

Practice Gratitude—Especially When You Can't See Your Blessings

I decided long ago that no matter what happened in my life, I would always try to find a way to be happy about it. Before I discovered this marvelous way of thinking and experienced the benefits of gratitude, I'd been allowing myself to live my life blindly and miserably. I was a young fashion model who had won beauty contests and pageants, and I had a successful career in sales and interior design. I was well-traveled and had money in the bank, a great place to live, a fabulous job, lots of amazing friends, a wonderful and loving family, and an exciting social life. In short, I had a life that (on the exterior) most people would envy, but, ironically, I was also, without a doubt, the most miserable I'd ever been. I had zero gratitude.

I would spend my days focusing on everything I *didn't* have. If I was chosen to attend a casting or audition, I would tell myself how bad I looked, berating myself for not being thin enough or pretty enough. I'd engage in negative self-talk about how much I'd failed at the casting requirements. I wasn't grateful for my clothes, my car, my watch, or my purse. I wanted the most up-to-date fashion designs, a fabulous sports car, the latest Cartier watch, all the designer handbags, and anything else that caught my eye in the newest copy of *Vogue*. There was no end to my dissatisfaction—or my complaints.

We've all known someone who seems to have everything going for them but still remains miserable, whether it's someone famous or someone we know personally. Despite having money, cars, fame, success, marriages (often several), or the hottest dates, they are clearly unhappy as they chase after the latest thing. They may appear "successful" on the outside, but inside, they're a vacuum of misery. These are people who desperately need a gratitude practice—people who need to focus on the many things they *do* have.

There are nights when I can't sleep because my mind is racing with the many things I need to take care of: the multiple projects I have to finish, the issues I need to take care of for my husband and children, the work problems that require a timely solution, and the long-term worries that I wish I could resolve. On these nights, it has helped me to pause and make a mental gratitude list. Now, when my mind is spinning, I think of twenty things I am grateful for. I spend a few moments focusing on each one and how it makes me feel. There have even been a couple of times when I've gotten close to one hundred things before nodding off. Though usually, I'm tired by the time I've thought of twenty things. I've found that creating a mental gratitude list is the best way to fall asleep each night.

Making a conscious effort to live in a state of gratitude will help you feel better about your life, and, as a result, you will make better choices. I like to say, "With gratitude, the things that you appreciate, appreciate."

Gratitude in Every Moment

Gratitude is a central element of Buddhism, Christianity, Judaism, Islamic, and many other belief systems. Many people say daily prayers to thank God for their blessings, including repeating specific prayers such as the Modeh Ani, a short Hebrew prayer thanking God for life. When we live in gratitude, we focus on being grateful for what we have, and we are not thinking about lack but focusing on abundance.

There are many ways to express gratitude, which we can find in every moment of our day. I am writing this chapter from my kitchen counter, and as I look out of my window, I can see a bird making a nest in one of my gutters. While it's not an ideal situation for the function of a gutter (and maybe not great for the bird if we have a big rainstorm), the beauty I get to witness each day creates a spark of gratitude, as this incredible little bird brings each tiny piece of dried grass or twig to carefully form its nest, where it will lay its eggs and bring baby birds into the world.

Right now, I'm also drinking a delicious cup of hot Colombian coffee that my hot Colombian husband made me. We have been together for twenty-three years, and I still find him hot. We have a fabulous marriage and partnership, and I am eternally grateful for him, his love, and his unwavering support of me and all of my projects. That's another example of gratitude. As I drink my coffee each morning, I take a moment to think of how grateful I am for the chain of events that had to occur to bring this coffee to me, all the way from the mountains of Colombia.

There is so much power in gratitude. When we focus on being grateful, we are not living in the past or manufacturing fearful thoughts about the future. We are simply living in the present moment and being thankful for it.

Emily Fletcher, the founder of Ziva, a well-known meditation training site, says that gratitude is a "natural antidepressant." The effects of gratitude, when practiced daily, can induce the same response as medication. It produces a feeling of long-lasting happiness and contentment. When we express—and receive—gratitude, our brain releases dopamine and serotonin, the two crucial neurotransmitters responsible for positive emotions, and they enhance our mood immediately, making us feel happy. By consciously practicing gratitude every day, we can help these neural pathways to strengthen and ultimately create a permanent, grateful, positive nature within ourselves.[15]

Starting Your Own Gratitude Practice

To practice gratitude, we need to be fully present and give our complete attention to the present moment, guiding our thoughts to notice and appreciate the things we are most grateful for. If you haven't already, commit to starting a gratitude practice today. Find a notebook or journal, open it up, and write down just *one* thing you are grateful for. Then take a moment to think about that one thing and what it means to you. Then, add more things to your list—and repeat as needed. Going forward, write down at least ten things for which you are grateful until you have covered everything that you can think of. As you do this, reflect on that thing's importance in your life. Feel free to add items to your gratitude journal any time you think of them or when you need a mood boost. You can even carry your gratitude journal with you throughout the day as a reminder to look for the positive things in your life.

Remember, *what you appreciate, appreciates.* The more you practice this way of thinking, the easier it gets. Gratitude is like a muscle. When you use it regularly, it will grow and get stronger. As you add items you're thankful for to your list, your gratitude will magnify. Initially, it may be challenging to find things you're grateful for, or you may see the glass as half empty instead of half full. But as you work on strengthening your gratitude practice, you'll begin to find more and more things to appreciate in your life.

Here are some other ways to strengthen your gratitude practice:

- Send thank-you notes to the people in your life who you're grateful for or write a letter to someone you admire or someone who has influenced your life in a positive way.
- Create a gratitude jar and fill it with handwritten notes of things you are grateful for.
- Create a daily affirmation of gratitude that you say each morning and each evening as you awaken and as you fall asleep. It can be something as simple as: "Today, I am grateful for my health and the opportunities that today will bring." Make your affirmation personal and meaningful to you.
- If you spend most of the day indoors, take time to go outside and take in the beauty of nature, being present in the moment and appreciating all

you see and experience. Try a meditation/gratitude walk during your lunch break instead of scrolling through your phone.

- Take a moment each morning and evening to say a gratitude prayer or affirmation silently to yourself. This will only take a few minutes, but the benefits you reap from this exercise will bring lasting happiness.
- Spread gratitude to others by verbally telling them why you are grateful for them. Remember that gratitude is contagious, and they may do the same for others!

No matter what you choose to do, know that it's important to make gratitude something you practice daily and schedule a few moments into each day to practice your favorite gratitude exercises.

Every individual has the ability to practice gratitude. It's not just reserved for the naturally calm, zen types. My husband, for example, has zero patience. I joke to our children that when God was giving out patience, their dad was at the back of the queue, and because he couldn't be bothered waiting around, he didn't get any. He hates being stuck in traffic and could probably kill someone for using a gas-powered leaf blower loudly on a Sunday morning when he's sitting on the deck reading his paper. But over the last decade, mainly through my insistence, he's learned to use these moments to practice gratitude. He now comes home after battling traffic with a smile on his face because, during his commute, he thinks about his appreciation for his family, his success, his ability to drive, his house, and his health. It is a small but radical shift in his thinking that will probably add years to his life by decreasing his stress level. (I'll be honest with you, though. We're still working on the leaf blowers, especially if several are running at the same time. But at least now he can look up and smile at me when those engines start running.)

If you find yourself struggling to think of what to be grateful for (which is very common for anyone starting their gratitude practice), here's a list of helpful prompts:

- What do you like the most about yourself?
- What is the best compliment you've ever received, and what did you appreciate about it?
- Who has been there for you when you needed them?
- Have you ever received kindness from a stranger?
- Do you have any employees or coworkers for whom you are grateful?
- Have any of your family members recently done somcthing for you—big or small?
- What is the best film you've ever seen or the best book you've ever read, and what did you like about it?
- What is your favorite view?
- Have you recently gone for a walk in nature?
- Is there an aspect of your health you're grateful for?
- Think about your mind and how beautiful it can be when it's filled with good thoughts. Does that bring warmth or another positive feeling to your heart?

- Place your hand on your heart and think of the thing you are most grateful for.
- Think of your life and all the things you have overcome, then take a moment to be grateful for your courage and strength in those moments.
- Reflect on how beautiful it is to have a place where you can take the time to read this book—and others like it—and the wisdom you can gain.
- Thank people and spread joy—it's contagious! Thank your server or barista verbally for their service, not just with a tip. Thank your bus, cab, or Uber driver by making eye contact and telling them what you appreciated about the journey.
- Treat your employees and coworkers with respect and appreciation, thanking them often for all they do.
- Take five minutes to phone or text a friend or family member you haven't spoken to in a while just to let them know how much they mean to you.
- Thank yourself for the work you're now doing on yourself, for yourself.
- Buy yourself some flowers or a sweet treat to show yourself gratitude.
- Write a letter to yourself detailing all the things you're grateful for in your life.
- Write a letter of gratitude to a friend or give them a small gift.
- Thank a stranger today for a small act of kindness, like opening a door for you or letting you go in front of them in line.

Gratitude is like a magic wand. When you wave it, you can feel your stress and anxiety begin to lift as you focus on the beautiful areas of your life and all you have to be grateful for. Go out of your way to show the people in your life how grateful you are for them and notice how this increases your day-to-day happiness and strengthens your relationships. And remember, *what you appreciate, appreciates.*

7

BE THE CHANGE

Make Your Actions Congruent with Your Words

Bravery is when you speak up and
speak out for what is right.
—Malala Yousafzai[16]

I grew up in a small town in Yorkshire, England. My mother was born and raised there, and my father was a British national born in Egypt. By the time my dad was eighteen, he had traveled most of the world. He spoke several languages and had seen a great deal in his young life. My mother, on the other hand, had not traveled very much because her father died in his thirties, leaving my grandmother a widow with three young children.

The last time my mother saw her father, he was standing by the fireplace, warming his hands as she headed upstairs to bed. "Goodnight, Mary," he called out. She stopped halfway up the stairs and turned around. "Goodnight, Dad," she replied, not knowing that this would be the last time she would ever see him alive, or that this would be their last interaction. Later, my mother would tell me how grateful she was that she'd gotten to smile at him and tell him goodnight before he died. It gave her solace when she thought of him in the years that followed. And of course, she passed that lesson down, making it a point to teach me never to go to bed upset with someone because you never know if that will be the last time you'll see them.

Although my grandfather had never traveled outside of England, he knew a lot about the world. In fact, after he died, my mother found a picture of Gandhi that he carried in his wallet with the phrase "Be the change." Here was a man who had only ever traveled within a few hundred miles from the place he was born, but his inspiration came from someone on the other side of the world.

I have always loved that expression "Be the change"—it is both simple and powerful. For most of my adult life, I have tried to live by it. I taught it to my children and have used it to inspire others. It is written on a sign above my entryway door so that every time I go out into the world, I will remember it.

Walking the Talk

I was raised to know the difference between *doing* and *being*. People will talk the talk, but often their actions are not congruent with their words. As the saying goes, "Words are cheap." Actions and accountability are what matters. My mother was the perfect example of someone who lived by Gandhi's mantra. She shared with us children stories of growing up during and after the Second World War—stories of survival, bravery, kindness, and humanity, as well as stories of the atrocities that can happen when an evil or self-serving leader gains power. The British people, including my mother, suffered extreme poverty when the Nazi forces tried to starve them into submission by blocking the delivery of shipments from America and having submarines attack shipping vessels. Because most of the infrastructure had been used for war efforts, Britain had a scarcity of food and household items. Basic necessities were in short supply or completely unavailable.

However, the British people showed great courage and endurance. I grew up listening to many wonderful, true tales of the grit and defiance displayed during those times. My family never had very much money growing up, but my mother always taught us to share what we had, insisting my siblings and I share with those who were less fortunate. How my mother was able to do this with the small amount she had was unbelievable. Yet, she was generous to a fault, often going without so she could give to others.

Even though my parents were raising seven children on one salary, they donated countless hours of time to people in need. They gave money to missionaries throughout the world to aid in healthcare, education, social justice, and economic development. My mother encouraged all of her children to raise funds to sponsor children living in poverty in Africa. My siblings and I each had a card with a beautiful photo of a child from a remote village in Africa. We loved raising and sending money to these children. We would sell our old toys and clothes at garage sales to make extra money to give away. (In England, they are called *jumble sales.*) In addition, my mother would feed, clothe, and take care of many poor children we knew from the church and the neighborhood. There was always someone in need she was helping.

As a child, I was naturally a little bit reluctant to give any of my belongings away. It was not until my adult life that I began to realize the value of my mother's example. One of her favorite sayings, "You are only poor when you want more than you have," stays with me to this day.

Growing up, I saw the happiness my mother received from giving to others. When I first became involved in charitable causes, I found that there were so many that needed my help, so many that spoke to me. After a while, I started to feel overwhelmed about where to focus my efforts. After some reflection, I chose several causes that I felt were closest to my heart, where I thought I could do the most good. (I've provided a list of these charities at the end of the book.) Now I enjoy giving to and volunteering with these organizations.

Sometimes, it can be challenging to know what causes to champion—especially in our ideologically fragmented world. Whenever I find myself faced with a person with whom I disagree, or someone who has different political viewpoints than I do, I like to consider the following questions: *What information has this person been fed to believe the things they're currently believing? What is their unique story? How can I work for positive change and have meaningful dialogue without fighting with this person? How am I to advocate for the things that are important to me—like protecting our planet and helping secure rights for our LGBTQ community, minority communities, women, and children—without getting caught up in political arguments?*

At some point, I believe we all have to put disagreements aside and just do what's right: Be kind to people. Stand up for others. Help those who are in need. I find it impossible to believe that a person who considers themselves religious can lack compassion for another group of humans. It's never wrong to put yourself in the shoes of others and have some compassion.

Walk in Someone Else's Shoes

The immigration debate in this country is a prime example of how a topic has become unnecessarily politicized. There have always been and always will be people seeking refuge in safer countries. As an immigrant myself, I understand the difficulties involved in becoming a legal citizen of the United States. The naturalization process is quite long and complicated (as I believe it should be) and requires many steps. First, you must be checked medically by an immigration-approved medical doctor (to make sure you are not bringing any diseases into the country). For women, that includes a gynecological exam. Then, for ninety days, the FBI does a full background check on you to make sure you don't pose any kind of danger to America. It took me five years to get my legal residency and fifteen years to become a citizen. This was no easy feat, and I cried with pride the day I finally got my citizenship.

We *all* want to live in a welcoming and safe country. While we shouldn't freely support criminal enterprises, such as bringing drugs and contraband into the country, we must improve and enlarge the pathways to enter the US legally. We are a country of immigrants, so it seems odd to me that so many people whose ancestors entered the US only a generation or so ago now want to close the door to legal and fair immigration.

My Colombian American husband has provided healthcare for hundreds of Latino immigrants, and many he has treated for free because they could not afford health insurance. He tells me that, *without exception*, all of his Latino patients have been hardworking, law-abiding individuals who are truly grateful to be in the US. When he volunteered in Haiti in the mid-1990s, he and his team treated eight hundred people in a period of four days. They had to work in the heat with only battery-operated fans. What struck him the most was the massive crowd of people who were patiently waiting for care. They were standing in a long line, nobody pushing in front of the next person, nobody complaining about the wait or the heat or the limited care that they were waiting to receive. In fact, two of the women in line went into labor while they were waiting. My husband had to leave the patient he was currently treating and rush over to a tree, where one of the women was squatting down to deliver her baby. Even in such a desperate state, she had not tried to make her way to the front of the line.

A lot of people who live in the first world (myself included) have zero clue what life must be like for those born in places with such limited resources or what it would be like to grow up in a country devastated by war or violence. In the time since my husband's medical mission trip to Haiti, the political situation in that country has become so dangerous that people have been forced to leave the region just to stay alive. Sadly, we can't help the whole world, but I do feel strongly that law-abiding, hardworking people who want to create a better life for themselves or who are escaping violence and war should be allowed compassionate immigration visas into the safety of more developed countries.

Studies have shown that immigrants tend to be entrepreneurial, and, on the whole, they contribute positively to their communities in many ways—economically, socially, politically, and culturally.

Albert Einstein, for example, the father of modern physics, was granted US citizenship in 1940 after escaping Nazi Germany. The German government had passed laws barring Jewish citizens from holding any official positions, including teaching at universities. Einstein brought his knowledge to America and continued his career at Princeton University. While lecturing at Lincoln University in Pennsylvania, a historically Black college, he was awarded an honorary degree. He later joined the National Association for the Advancement of Colored People (NAACP) in Princeton, where he campaigned for civil rights. Einstein considered racism America's "worst disease."[17]

Another immigrant who helped shape the United States was Madeleine Albright, who was born in the country formerly known as Czechoslovakia two years before World War II and was able to come to the US after Hitler's defeat. After earning her PhD at Columbia University, Albright officially entered the political world as a National Security Council liaison in the Carter administration. In 1993, she was nominated to be the American ambassador to the United Nations. Soon after, she joined the Clinton administration as secretary of state, where she oversaw foreign policy during the conflicts in Bosnia and Herzegovina. In addition to her countless honorary degrees and awards, President Obama awarded Albright the Presidential Medal of Freedom in 2012.[18]

Einstein and Albright are just two examples of immigrants who dramatically improved America as a whole, but there are thousands more who have made a difference in our world through their hard work, dedication, and good character. Acts of kindness to others remind us of our shared humanity. When we extend compassion to people whose lives have been marked by hardship or displacement, we open our own hearts to grace.

Living Your Values

The *being* part of "Being the change" is both internal and external. Aside from putting yourself in another person's shoes and truly being kind and compassionate on the inside, *being* is also about how we live out loud—about the actions we take to show that we care about the things in our world. Think of it as telling the story of what you care about.

"Be the change" could be the mantra of two other extraordinary women in our world: Greta Thunberg and Malala Yousafzai.

Greta Thunberg is a Swedish environmental activist who has challenged world leaders to take immediate action to mitigate the effects of human-caused climate change. She began her work at age fifteen and quickly gained worldwide attention for her efforts and dedication to saving our planet. Malala Yousafzai is a Pakistani women's education activist, film and television producer, and the winner of the 2014 Nobel Peace Prize, which she was awarded at the age of seventeen, making her the youngest Nobel laureate in history and the only Pashtun to receive a Nobel Prize. She is best known for her work as a human rights advocate for the education of women and children in her native land, a place where the Taliban has banned girls from attending school. Though we can't all be the next Greta Thunberg or Malala Yousafzai, we can learn from their examples and find fulfillment in helping others—and model being the change. Anyone, regardless of their circumstances, can become an agent of positive transformation by taking small but consistent actions, having a mindset of service, and leading by example with kindness, compassion, and strength.

A woman who has inspired me locally to be the change began her organization here in Aspen, Colorado. Gina Murdock founded her nonprofit organization, Lead with Love, out of a deep desire to shift cultural paradigms from fear-based systems to love-centered living. Lead with Love is about healing ourselves so we can heal the world. After witnessing the stress, disconnection, and disillusionment plaguing modern life, even in affluent and spiritually conscious communities, Gina recognized the urgent need for mindful leadership rooted in compassion and service. She envisioned Lead with Love as a platform to gather changemakers, wellness leaders, and seekers to co-create a world that prioritizes healing, justice, and well-being for all.

For Gina, love isn't simply a soft ideal—it's a powerful force, one that's capable of transforming individuals, organizations, and entire systems. Gina lives by a simple but profound truth: *Change starts from within.* In a world overwhelmed by crisis, inequality, and mental health epidemics, it's easy to feel paralyzed. However, Gina believes that every person has the power to be a catalyst for transformation, beginning with themselves. She believes that the real revolution happens when you look inward and ask, *How am I contributing to the problem, and how can I become part of the solution?* Through the Lead with Love platform, she began a global movement that empowers others to heal their own hearts so they can serve the world more effectively. By offering workshops, events, retreats, summits, and community initiatives, Gina invites others to "be the change" and align their actions with their values.[19]

THE THINGS THAT MATTER

What are the things that deeply matter to you? Take some time to reflect on these questions:

- What do you care about deeply? What issues are close to your heart?

- What kind of world do you want to live in, and how can you help create that?
- What can you do in your own life to work for positive change?
- What is the change you want to see, and can you find ways to get involved?
- Real change often begins at the most immediate level in your own community. What strengths, skills, or resources do you possess to help make the change?

The Power of ONE

Often people hesitate to get involved because they feel that their contribution is too small or too insignificant, but remember: Change starts with the power of ONE. Whether it's fighting climate change, advocating for social justice, supporting women's and children's issues, or helping the homeless, change can start at a local level.

No matter where you decide to focus your efforts, always listen actively so you can engage with people and learn their stories. Listening is so much more powerful than speaking. And remember to be patient—all change, including social change, takes time. Treat all people with kindness, including yourself. Lead by example. If you want to foster a culture of kindness, be kind. Leading by example means embodying the values you want to see in others and in the world. Be consistent.

Consider donating to a cause you care about or becoming a volunteer. Giving your time is one of the simplest yet most effective ways to make a difference. Start in your local community by asking around and seeing what opportunities are available. Grassroots efforts can grow into large movements. Surround yourself with like-minded people who share your passion and enthusiasm and also want to make a difference. Partner with local organizations and community leaders to help create safe spaces where people feel heard, valued, and empowered.

Remember, knowledge is a powerful tool. Educating others not only spreads awareness but also empowers them to take action in their own lives. Share what you know and create opportunities for others to learn along with you.

Never underestimate the power of ONE. Your voice, your dedication, and your work can make a difference. And remember, it is not always the grandest gestures that bring about the most changes. Sometimes, the most impactful actions are the small but consistent efforts we make—a smile, a kind word, helping a neighbor, and standing up for people who are being treated unfairly.

Being a true leader involves empowering other people to also lead. Can you encourage those around you to help, to share their time and talents, and to take ownership of the change they want to see? To effect change, you don't need to possess extraordinary wealth, power, or influence. All you need is passion, empathy, and persistence. Every small act of kindness, every step toward justice, and every effort to improve the world and the lives of others makes a difference.

8

UNRAVELING THE TAPESTRY

Break Problems Down into Small, Actionable Steps

The journey of a thousand miles
begins with a single step.
—*Lao Tzu*

The earliest known tapestry was a linen work of art created in ancient Egypt and found in the tombs of Tutankhamun. Tapestries have been woven throughout the world for centuries from the grand medieval tapestries that hang in palaces to small works of art that decorate people's living rooms. While finished tapestries appear intricate and fragile, they are created by physically demanding spinning and detailed weaving. Some tapestries were created in reverse, with the pattern on the opposite side of where the weaver was working so that when all of the intricate work was done, a beautiful image was revealed. If the weaver made a mistake during this arduous process, they had to cut one of the strings and begin to pull it out by hand. Slowly but surely, as they pulled on the string, the entire image would unravel bit by bit. Why am I going on and on about tapestries? Well, this tightly woven fabric serves as a beautiful metaphor for overcoming life's problems.

A good friend of mine, the great German ski legend Klaus Obermeyer, used to say, "Look at a problem like you are unraveling a tapestry." Klaus had an amazing outlook on life. He escaped Germany during the Second World War and was exposed to a great deal of suffering. He decided early on not to let his difficult circumstances get the better of him. He determined to always believe in the best outcome, look on the bright side of every circumstance, and have the best possible attitude no matter what the situation. He encouraged me to look at problems like a tapestry, with all of their intricacies, the threads interwoven by painstaking detailed work. I have relied on the power of this metaphor many times in my life. I think about it whenever I have a difficult task ahead of me or when I'm faced with a problem that seems impossible. I begin by breaking the challenge down as I've learned that if something that seems daunting or overwhelming is broken down into small, actionable steps, it becomes a lot easier to tackle.

Splashing in Puddles

Most people imagine their problems as a big balloon filled with water, positioned directly above their heads and following them around like a dark cloud. They see it as a ticking time bomb, ready to explode at any moment and drown them. They're terrified to look up and face their problems, so they live most of their lives trying to dodge them or avoid them or pretending they don't exist. If this is your situation, try doing the following visualization exercise.

First, imagine you are a child, living totally carefree in this world. Life is fun and full of surprises. Your problem still exists, but this time you see it as a giant red water balloon bouncing up and down on the floor in front of you. You run up to it with a huge smile on your face. *How fun!* you think. *This is awesome!* You just know that something extraordinary is about to happen. Then you reach into your pocket and pull out a sharp knitting needle. The shining tip of it glistens, and you chuckle a little bit to yourself.

With glee and reckless abandon, you pounce forward and prepare to stab the balloon with your needle. *How incredibly lucky I am to be the one who gets to do this!* you tell yourself. Just as you are about to pierce the rubber of the balloon, you think about how wet you might get when the bubble bursts. Yes, you will get wet, but you're dressed in your Wellies and raincoat, so you know you'll be fine.

You swiftly proceed to hit the center of the balloon with your pin. With one loud and immense swoosh, the water splashes all over the floor and the room. It collects in small puddles. You step forward and, with childlike glee, begin to jump up and down, splashing the water in each puddle. Instead of drowning you, the water has now become something you have complete control over. One by one, you walk over to each separate puddle on the floor and splash up and down in it, making it smaller and smaller as you stomp around.

I have just described how to tackle 99 percent of life's problems. It's only a puddle—one that we can have fun jumping up and down in before it becomes a smaller puddle and eventually disappears. Break down each problem and address it like a small puddle of water.

Yet many times in life, our problems overwhelm us, becoming so big that we feel too paralyzed to address them. But try to look at your problem like a balloon filled with water, one that you can burst and make into smaller puddles. That will enable your feeling of powerlessness to disappear and be replaced by the confidence of taking action. And remember—if you can solve a problem with time or money, then it's not really a problem.

Now let's do a little exercise. We're going to look at your problem and try to find its root cause. First, let's figure out what you're facing. Ask yourself the following questions:

- *Am I suffering from financial stress because of debt or unemployment?*
- *Do I have health issues that I need to address?*
- *Am I having problems at work?*
- *Do I lack purpose or direction?*
- *Is time management a challenge for me?*
- *Is my house always messy because I have too much stuff?*
- *Am I disorganized?*

- *Is my living space always untidy because I don't clean up after myself?*
- *Have I gotten speeding tickets because I'm often in a hurry and drive too fast?*
- *Am I having problems at work because I'm often late or don't use my time well?*
- *Am I having relationship problems because the other person thinks I don't care about them?*
- *Do I have issues with drugs or alcohol that have created problems I need to address?*
- *Do I have financial problems, such as overspending or having unpaid bills?*

These are some of the most common problems that people have, but like all problems, breaking down their solutions into small, actionable steps is a proven way to begin conquering them. Let's say, for example, that you have a room full of junk you need to clear out. The clutter has been there for years, and every time you look at that room, you feel sick knowing that one day you're going to have to address the giant mess. The only thing that brings you any relief is keeping the door closed, with everything out of sight and out of mind.

Right now, tell yourself you're going to get started—you're going to clean that room. And remind yourself that by breaking down this daunting task into small, actionable steps, you will feel less overwhelmed. Make a list of the steps you're going to take before you do anything else. Spend time on this list so it's clear in your mind how the project is going to be executed. Having a specific plan will help you feel more inspired to finish the problem.

A STEP-BY-STEP GARAGE-CLEANING PLAN

1. Write your ten-step actionable plan.
2. Spend up to thirty minutes on Instagram, Pinterest, or TikTok getting inspiration for an aesthetically pleasing clean and organized garage. (Set a timer so you don't spend too much time on this step!)
3. Go to the store and purchase bags, boxes, Post-it notes or cardstock, tape, a package of Sharpies, or any other supplies you may need.
4. Fill up a big water bottle (you're going to need some hydration!), open the garage door, and head right into the chaos.
5. Mentally divide the items in the garage into categories, then write the names of each category on pieces of cardstock or Post-it notes. For example: *tools; gardening equipment; paint; camping supplies; kids' stuff; items to sell; items to donate; junk to throw away.*
6. Place each label in a different area, and then begin to gather every item that fits in a specific category. As you're doing this, decide which section of the garage will be used for each category.
7. Slowly put all of the items you need back into place, keeping only what you know you will use and getting rid of everything else.
8. Pack up the car with everything you want to get rid of or donate, then head for Goodwill, another

donation center, or the dump. (And make sure you return home with an empty vehicle!)

9. When you're back home, you can keep doing more organizing until you're happy with the way your garage looks. (Don't be afraid to declutter even more at this point!)
10. After you've finished, smile at how far you've come on a project that previously paralyzed you—you've done an amazing job!

You can apply this plan to any area of your life. Take any problem you have, break it down into ten actionable steps, and then work at each step until your goal is achieved. You'll feel a lot less overwhelmed, and you'll be able to accomplish things you'd previously imagined were impossible.

Eat the Frog First

Another helpful problem-solving technique is to prioritize which problems you need to address first and then create a clear action plan for *when* to address those problems. I like Mark Twain's advice that if you have to eat a live frog, do it first thing in the morning, and nothing worse will happen to you for the rest of the day.

This "eat the frog first" strategy is a prioritization and productivity method used to help people identify their most difficult tasks. It has helped me so much throughout my life, and I still use it on a regular basis.

In my earlier life, I would often avoid the most difficult project by putting it off and allowing meaningless, unimportant busywork to fill my day, while the "live frog" task was sitting, staring me in the face. Now, when I can, I get the hard stuff over and done with *first.* This achieves two things: It gets the most difficult task out of the way, and it gives me a great sense of achievement once the task has been accomplished. Having the most difficult thing on your to-do list behind you frees your mental energy and promotes self-confidence. You can then sail through the rest of the day knowing you've already dealt with the problem that was weighing the heaviest on you.

"I Don't Have Enough Time!"

It's easy to convince ourselves we don't have time to complete the things we've been avoiding. Once I've made my list of priorities, I like to divide it into three categories: *now*, *later*, and *sometime*. You don't have to do everything today. Writing down a problem on a list and having a plan as to *when* it will get addressed, knowing I'll get to it at some point, always helps me get going. I can see that it will eventually get done, and usually the feeling of urgency vanishes.

My sister, a busy mother of twins, schedules her day in blocks. From getting the kids on the early-morning school bus, to allowing herself time for yoga and exercise, to homework and dinner, her day is divided into many different sections of time. She starts her day early, at 6 a.m., giving herself thirty minutes to make coffee and breakfast for herself and the kids. She likes for them all to sit down together in the morning and eat, which is something I never did—I was always too busy racing around! My sister gives herself thirty minutes to an hour for everything she needs to accomplish, and she seems to get a lot done by using this method.

With modern technology, we all have easy access to stopwatches and timers on our phones. When my children were little, I would set the timer for twenty minutes, and we would run around and see how much stuff we could pick up before the alarm went off. It was a fun game that worked wonders at getting the toy room cleaned up. My daughter, who's now an adult, still uses twenty-minute time blocks to put laundry away or get her closet organized.

Rome wasn't built in a day, so know that if you are feeling overwhelmed, you aren't alone. Keep telling yourself, *That way of thinking is in my past, and it doesn't have to be this way going forward.* If there is a problem or issue that feels too big or overwhelming for you to tackle or a goal that seems impossible, take the time to break it down into actionable steps. Be realistic with yourself about what needs to be done *now* and what can wait. If you feel like you have multiple problems that need to be addressed *right now*, try to rank them by ones that will give you the most immediate benefit, whether that's a health benefit, a financial benefit, or a personal benefit. This will help you determine which problem has priority, and then you can get going on breaking it down into steps.

Ask yourself, *What is the one thing I can do today to address this monster of a problem?* Be kind to yourself as you work through your list, taking time to reflect and look back at what you've already accomplished. Then blast some of your favorite music or listen to an interesting podcast as you begin your work. You could also invite a friend or family member over to help you, and then do something nice for them in return.

Feel your problem-solving muscles begin to strengthen as you work through your lists. The following suggestions will help you not feel so overwhelmed:

- **Pause and Breathe:** Take a moment to breathe deeply. This can help calm your mind and body, making it easier to think clearly.
- **Break It Down:** Identify what's overwhelming you and break it down into smaller, more manageable tasks. Focus on one thing at a time instead of trying to tackle everything at once.
- **Prioritize:** Determine which tasks are the most urgent or important. Use a priority matrix (*now*, *later*, *sometime*) to help you focus on what truly matters.
- **Set Boundaries:** When you feel overwhelmed, learn to say no to additional responsibilities. Protecting your personal time is crucial.
- **Seek Support:** Talk to someone you trust about your feelings. Sometimes, sharing your thoughts with a friend can lighten the load.
- **Practice Self-Care:** Engage in activities that help you relax and recharge, whether that's exercising, reading, spending time in nature, or another favorite pursuit.

- **Establish a Routine:** Create a daily routine to provide structure and predictability, which can help reduce feelings of chaos.
- **Limit Distractions:** Identify those things that distract you from achieving your goal and try to minimize them. This might mean turning off notifications or creating a dedicated workspace.
- **Focus on the Present:** Practice mindfulness techniques to ground yourself in the present moment. As you engage in your daily tasks, try to get into the feeling of *flow*, when your mind is not focused on the past or the future, and you are not worried about time but are actively engaged in the current task, allowing yourself to easily transition from one thing to the next.

Remember, when we look at a problem like an intricate or complicated tapestry that we just need to start unraveling one section at a time and break it down into actionable, manageable steps, we will no longer feel immobilized by it. We know that once we begin to pull at and undo just one of the strings, the whole damn thing will eventually unravel. And then we have the freedom to create something new and beautiful.

9

YOU DO YOU

Stop Caring About What Others Think

Don't dim your light just to fit in
around others; seek those who shine,
and your light can be brighter still.
—*Kari Wells*

I was super excited when I found out that I had been chosen to be a cast member on the Bravo network show *Married to Medicine*. This was a new reality TV show that, I was told, was going to be a medical documentary series. It would highlight the lives of six affluent women from Atlanta and its surrounding communities who were all connected through the medical field. The show, according to the producers, was going to be very different from other reality shows airing at that time. Some reality shows of that era had been receiving negative press for fights and drama, but this show was supposed to be different—or at least, that's how the producers described it. *Married to Medicine*—which featured two women who were doctors and four women who were professionals who happened to be married to doctors—was supposed to be based on the drama of the medical field, not the drama between individuals.

The moment we began filming, I started to notice some major red flags. The first event was a get-to-know-each-other party for all of the cast members at the home of the show's co-producer Mariah Huq. During the evening, things got a little heated between me and one of the other cast members, Quad Webb-Lunceford, the young wife of a psychiatrist. I accidentally called her (now ex) husband a *psychologist* instead of a *psychiatrist*. This was a simple mistake on my part, but she reacted to it as though I'd eaten one of her adorable pet Yorkshire terriers. It was the most pathetic display of overacting I had ever seen, laced with several mouthfuls of profanity.

From that point on, things went from bad to worse. The breaking point of the show came for me when two of my fellow castmates, Mariah and Toya, two beautiful wives of doctors, had a full-blown fistfight at an elegant black-tie event I was hosting at my home. (I later referred to it as the "black eye" event.) Neither I nor any of the guests who were present that night could believe the violent hairpulling and punching that went on. For what seemed like an eternity, the two women dragged each other back and forth, fingers tightly grasping each other's weaves like they were clutching desperately to lifeboats from the sinking *Titanic*.

The fight scene drama resulted in impressive ratings as a record number of viewers around the globe tuned in. Unfortunately, it became one of the most talked-about scenes *ever* on reality TV, and everyone online had an opinion about it. Being that the rest of the cast was African American, I became known as "that white woman whose home got trashed." I could no longer step outside my door without everyone asking me about it. It was not quite the fame I was seeking—and definitely not what I'd signed up for. To this day, twelve years later, I am still wrongly accused of kicking the fighting duo out of my house.

Looking back, I can see all the signs were there, but due to my lack of experience with reality TV combined with my enthusiasm for new adventures, I was unable to see the woods for the trees. I joke that I have "golden retriever syndrome," just like my adorable little golden pup. I dive into things with limitless passion, enthusiasm, and abandon like an energetic little puppy, always trusting it will work out for the best. This personality trait has served me well on many occasions, but from time to time, it's bitten me on the you-know-what when everything falls to pieces.

I had been somewhat naive and a little misled by one of *Married to Medicine's* creators. In my defense, in those early days of reality TV, nobody really knew the power the editors had. They could make you or break you with the click of their editing software. Viewers used to blindly trust that what they saw on their screens was unfolding in real time and in the order they were watching it. Today, most viewers know that what they're seeing is only about 50 percent real—the rest has been carefully created by film editors. In reality TV, it's the luck of the draw which character has a good or bad edit.

After the airing of the "black-eye" event episode, I felt like I was living a nightmare. I spent a few days crying, trying to determine how to move forward and figuring out how to overcome being wrongly depicted on the show. I wrote apology letters to all the guests who had attended the party because, being British, I felt fully responsible that it had happened in my home at an event I'd invited people to. I felt that while I was personally done being a cast member, I still had a contract to fulfill. As they say in the business, "The show must go on." So I finished out the season.

After the first season wrapped and I finished filming the reunion, I decided to remain a friend of the show and continued to appear on it for nine seasons. I wanted to have an opportunity to let viewers know who I really was—to let them see the *real* me, my authentic self, not the person I was portrayed to be in Season One. In the decade that followed, there was an avalanche of press about the show and a lot of interviews, TV articles, and blogs about it. Everybody had an opinion about Kari Wells of *Married to Medicine*. People would send me letters in the mail, DM me, text me, and even call my husband's medical practice, leaving me long and sometimes hateful messages. So many people around the world wanted to trash me or complain about me because of what they'd seen on the show.

On that fateful night of the infamous fight, I had hired a local cop to do security. Some of the guests who stormed out in disgust after watching the two ladies brawling told the officer he should go intervene. One of the guests apparently yelled, "You need to get in there—two ladies are killing each other!" The officer raced in just after five of the husbands, including mine, had managed to drag Mariah and Toya apart. Toya ran into my powder room, crying with embarrassment, where she was comforted by Dr. Simone. Mariah was left standing battered and disheveled. Not realizing who she was, the cop asked Mariah, the co-sponsor of the party, to leave. I had been standing in the kitchen in shock, watching it all unfold, so I didn't even witness her conversation with him. I was too busy telling the producers we were *done* here, all while things continued to escalate.

Later, when that episode came out, it looked like I was the one who had asked Mariah to leave, but that was never the case. I was the only white woman on the show, and some people depicted my out-of-context comment as racist. Later, my husband was caught on a hot mic privately telling me that he thought Mariah and her husband would probably get divorced, and that was it. We were officially hated by all of Mariah's bots and fans. Years later, Mariah and I apologized to each other for this major misunderstanding. All was forgiven, I'm delighted to report that Mariah and her husband, Aidan, are still married.

How to Care Less (About What Others Think)

Those ten years of filming served as a decade-long boot camp of slowly learning how to no longer give a damn about what other people thought of me. I felt like I'd completed a master class at an Ivy League business school: *How*

Not to Care About the Opinions of Others. I went from being devastated about little things to not giving a flying f#@K. I became a different person after those ten years spent on camera for the whole world to see. My resilience grew, my attitude about other people's opinions of me changed, and the experience made me a whole lot tougher.

It was an immensely freeing feeling to give up caring about things that, in the end, really didn't matter. I have always wanted to be liked and cared very much about pleasing others (which is very British of me). But now I have a solid group of friends who know and understand the *real* me, and that's all I need.

On our social media–obsessed planet, seeking outside approval is an integral part of the world we now live in. Most people have an online presence of some sort. Being obsessed with receiving likes and approval from others is the new norm.

The average person today can waste hours scrolling from one post to the next, and before they know it, they've fallen down the rabbit hole, with one link leading to another and then another until suddenly they realize they've spent an entire morning or afternoon watching YouTube videos of cats, catching up on the latest TikTok dance trends, and staring at the horror of Instagram shorts depicting angry "Karens" raging at Walmart employees.

On social media, it seems like everyone has an opinion and nobody is afraid to share it. Comments you would never dare say in person, even to an enemy, are casually spewed online. Nasty sentiments are published for all to see at the simple press of a button, and they never really disappear. Over the years, I've had people online say just about everything under the sun about me. One columnist wrote an article stating that I was born a man, another that my husband was gay, and someone even threatened my children. I'd never encountered such nastiness.

Online bullying can lead to a person suffering from intense depression or even committing suicide. There are cases when online posts have destroyed people's worlds, not to mention the many cases of extortion and blackmail when someone is threatened with the release of an intimate story or image.

People all over the world grow up worrying about what others think of their appearance or behavior, causing a lifetime of stress and anxiety. Every time someone shops at the grocery store, goes out to dinner, exercises at the gym or on the running trail, or spends time at school or work, a large percentage of what they're thinking about is what other people think of them. Now, I'm not saying you need to give up on your appearance, walk around naked, or wear a trash bag for an outfit. Nor am I saying you should say or do whatever you want and become an indifferent sociopath. But worrying about what other people—especially people you don't know—think of you is an enormous waste of your time and energy, and when all is said and done, do we ever *really* know what another person is thinking?

Growing up in England, I lived in what seemed to be the epicenter of worrying about what other people think of you. Women in England have been concerned with what other people think of them since prior to the tenth century, when they were raised to be, among other things, humble, self-disciplined, chaste, modest, dutiful, and pious. I grew up surrounded by British pomp and circumstance, mixed with a high dose of holier-than-thou Catholicism. I was trained in etiquette and social graces, and my sister was a certified etiquette coach who was hired by wealthy families to teach their children how to present themselves correctly for dinners and social events.

British people *always* worry about what other people think of them, and they detest complaining. The term "stiff upper lip" refers to the cultural trait of maintaining self-control, emotional restraint, and stoicism in the face of adversity, hardship, or difficult situations. The phrase captures the British ideal of handling personal or public challenges without complaint, visible distress, or other displays of emotion. The Brits are like Jedi Knights, holding it all inside with a perfect smile while quietly warning themselves, *What would people possibly think if I were to complain?*

During the Second World War, the phrase "Keep Calm and Carry On" became a point of pride for the British people, symbolizing resilience, endurance, and dignity in the face of bombings, food shortages, and many other hardships. This can be a wonderful and endearing trait, but on the flip side, it can lead to a lot of stress with the constant need for exhibiting self-restraint and always attempting to appear strong and resilient.

Being Your Authentic Self

When I first came to America, I was pleasantly surprised to discover that people often spoke their minds (often too much). This was strange, but I eventually found freedom in also behaving this way. The older I got, the more I found that when you are your true and authentic self, it gives the people you're around permission to feel comfortable being their authentic selves, and you're able to have deeper, more genuine relationships. This is when the magic happens. Beautiful souls will seek out other beautiful souls. So keep being your true, authentic self, and *your people* will find you.

These days, I have very little time for people who do not present their authentic selves. I lived in the American South for almost twenty years, rubbing elbows with other members of Atlanta high society. I used to feel like an imaginary glass screen was present between me and some of the women I socialized with, like they were holding back their true personalities, thoughts, and feelings in order to appear perfect and completely in control of their lives.

When I first met my husband, many of the doctors' wives he introduced me to would say negative things about me right to my face. Back then, I didn't have the confidence or courage to advocate for myself and express to them how their words made me feel. At my engagement party, one woman asked where my future husband and I had met. When I told her we'd met in Aspen, her super-friendly husband smiled and responded that he would like to go to Aspen. His wife, without missing a beat, shot daggers at him with her eyes and abruptly blurted out, "YOU are NOT going to Aspen! You might come back with someone like HER!"

A year later, when I was a couple of months pregnant, my husband and I were in Hawaii attending a medical conference at a beachfront resort. We were celebrating the wonderful news of our pregnancy with a group of my husband's doctor friends and their wives. This was before my belly was really showing, and I was wearing shorts, a crop top, and a small, gold bikini chain around my still-trim belly. One of the doctor's wives had just found out I was pregnant, and she wandered over to our group, looked at me with a face like a bulldog chewing on a wasp, and said loudly, "People will hate you if you dress like that when you're pregnant." I'd like to believe she meant it as a joke, but to me, so young and full of pregnancy hormones, it was like a slap in the face. I felt a lump in my throat as I tried to hold back my tears. I already was feeling like I didn't fit in with the group, and this certainly didn't help.

Had those hurtful events happened today, I would have had a lot to say. I would defend myself and make the women aware of their hurtful comments, or maybe I would just smile and laugh and let it roll off my back. I now realize that people see things not as they are but as *they* are, which means they interpret life by what is inside of them. People who make hateful comments are filled with hate. They are the ones who are insecure, and their comments often reflect their own insecurities, having very little to do with the recipient but *a lot* to do with them. As I now tell myself, *Your comments do not define me—but they do define* you, *as a person who needs to judge others.*

I have met insecure women who thought I was out to steal their man. They saw me as a threat who would take away their husband, fiancé, or boyfriend. They projected their insecurities toward me in the form of petty comments or dirty looks. I once had a woman rip up my business card and stuff it down my bra because she thought I was coming on to her ugly husband when, in fact, I was merely talking to him about the name of my production company. If I could go back in time, I would have the confidence to be honest and to say to these women, "Hey, don't worry. I'm not interested in your man. First of all, he's not my type, and second of all, even if he were, I'm not the type of woman to steal someone else's man."

If you find yourself worrying about the opinions of others to the point that it's affecting your happiness, here are some helpful tips:

- **Identify what's important to you.** When you're clear about your *own* values, the opinions of others matter a lot less. It's important to know your value as a person.
- **Practice self-care.** Be kind to yourself. Understand that everyone makes mistakes and has flaws. Embrace who you are without any judgment.
- **Limit your social media consumption.** I cannot stress how important this is. Social media can amplify comparisons and opinions. Take breaks or curate your feed to focus on positivity. This may mean deleting apps. Do it! Your mental health will thank you for it later.
- **Surround yourself with supportive people.** Spend time with those who uplift you and respect your choices rather than individuals who judge or criticize you.
- **Be aware of negative thoughts.** When you catch yourself worrying about the opinions of others,

question those thoughts. Are they really true, or are they just assumptions?

- **Focus on your goals.** Keep your attention on your personal goals and aspirations. This can help shift your focus away from others' perceptions.
- **Practice assertiveness.** Learn to express your thoughts and feelings clearly and confidently. This builds self-esteem and reduces concern about others' opinions.
- **Embrace your imperfections.** Understand that no one is perfect. Accepting your imperfections can lessen the fear of judgment from yourself and others.
- **Practice mindfulness and meditation.** Prioritizing these life-changing practices can help you stay grounded in the present and reduce worries about others' opinions.
- **Accept that you can't please everyone.** It's impossible to satisfy everyone, so focus on being true to yourself instead of trying to bend to the opinions of others.

Close your eyes and breathe deeply for a couple of breaths. Tell yourself that what others think—especially those you don't know well—doesn't matter. What does matter is knowing yourself, being comfortable with who you are, and embracing the amazing individual you are becoming. Then set an intention that today you will show up as your full, true, and authentic self.

10

BE RIGHT OR BE HAPPY

Let Go of Your Need to Control

When the choice is to be right
or to be kind, always make the
choice that brings peace.
—*Dr. Wayne Dyer*[20]

When it comes to conflict and communication, learning *how* to communicate is a skill that can make life immensely more peaceful and strengthen any relationship. You can be right or you can be happy, but you cannot be both. Letting go of being right is humbling, and it's also the path to peace. My husband jokingly says, "Happy wife, happy life," but choosing peace—and happiness—above being right has gotten us through some turbulent times in our twenty-three-plus-year marriage. It is not that I'm correct about all things; although I must admit I am most of the time (only joking . . . kind of). Still, my wise and wonderful husband and I have learned that insisting on being right only creates further disharmony, and continuously trying to prove your point to the other person not only takes a mental and physical toll but also adds fuel to an already heated argument. And in the end, does it really matter?

My father was a great man, but unfortunately, he thought he always had to be right. This is not to say he couldn't admit when he was wrong, but it was a rare event when he did. I blame it on the way he was raised by an overly protective Italian mother who adored him and insisted on doing everything for him. When my sweet mother got married to my father, she was only twenty-one years old, and the only marital advice she received from my Italian grandmother was, "If Frankie (my dad) says black is white, then you agree with him." My mother was young and naive, and she didn't like conflict, so throughout most of her marriage, she took the advice of her mother-in-law and agreed with my father, choosing peace over conflict and always being the one to give in and allow my dad to be correct.

As the youngest of seven siblings, I grew up with this parental dynamic, which I found infuriating. I was a fiery young child, a lot like my father, and in my youth, I often felt the need to prove I was right in order to validate my fragile self-worth. Whenever my mother bowed down to my dad's dominating ego, the young feminist in me would mentally stamp her foot. I wasn't aware that her calm non confrontational way, wasn't submission—it was quite strength, aimed at keeping peace in our home. I wanted to stick up for my adorable, kind, and loving mother, but I was too scared to open my mouth. My strict, military-trained father would never stand for any kind of disrespect, especially not from his children, and he was not afraid to spank us for any kind of behavior he associated with disobedience.

The physical punishment I experienced as a child continued until I was a teenager. It was then that I began to work on myself and discover aspects of my personality I wanted to change. Having a fragile ego that needed constant validation was definitely one of them. I didn't like acting this way; in fact, I viewed it as a character flaw, but it wasn't until I was an adult that I was able to let that go.

When I began to raise my own children, I wanted to do things differently than my parents had. Every parent wants to do what they feel is best for their offspring, and this can often be quite different from how they were raised, especially if they have experienced any form of dysfunction, which I definitely did in my family. I do not blame my father for hitting us children because he was raised in the era of "spare the rod, spoil the child," and he believed that if a parent *didn't* hit their children, they would actually harm them. Of course, we now know that's not true, but I believe my father did the best he could with what he had. He just didn't have the mental tools to handle things differently.

Sadly, for me and for some of my other siblings, this style of parenting completely broke our spirits. The National Institutes of Health now links physical punishment to a child's deficit of cognitive, behavioral, social, and emotional development.[21] A government study in Australia, involving over 160,000 children, found that physical punishment can have adverse outcomes for children's mental health and emotional challenges, creating lower cognitive ability, decreased self-esteem, more aggression, and increased antisocial behavior, as well as damaging the parent-child relationship. Stress from physical punishment can also negatively affect children's brain development.[22]

Kids learn from watching their parents. And parents who use physical discipline may be teaching their children to resolve conflicts with physical aggression. My husband and I, who were both punished physically as children, decided early on that there would be no spanking in our household. We both felt it had contributed to our own mental health challenges and personal struggles, and we wanted the cycle of abuse to end with our generation.

I distinctly recall one Thanksgiving when my son was six years old. He was an incredibly rambunctious child, and he often did not behave in a way that my father approved of. My parents were visiting us from England, and my sister and I had decided to do a big Thanksgiving dinner at her home. My sister had young twins at the time, and the house was quite lively with four children under age six running around.

This was the first time we'd all gotten together for Thanksgiving as a family since the holiday is not celebrated in England. My sister, mother, and I spent all day cooking, and we set a beautiful table for the ten of us. It was a wonderful occasion—both families together, my aging parents witnessing Thanksgiving traditions with their daughters, sons-in-law, and grandchildren.

Everybody knows the holidays can be stressful, and some of the most joyful occasions can easily be ruined with conflict. That Thanksgiving, as we all sat down to eat at this beautifully decorated table, laden with dishes that had taken an entire day to prepare, my six-year-old son, hungry and impatient from waiting, reached out to help himself to some food and spilled it on the table, making a mess. This infuriated my father. He allowed his anger to get the better of him and spanked his grandson's hand.

My young son had never been hit before, and he naturally burst into tears. Everybody at the table was shocked, and my husband was understandably mortified. Things went quickly downhill. My husband angrily got up from the table and took our crying son upstairs to console him, which further angered my father. I yelled at my father to *never* hit my child, and my mother burst into tears, quietly pleading with my father not to ever discipline the grandchildren again. This all happened before any of us had taken a bite of food or expressed what we were grateful for.

After that painful Thanksgiving dinner, my dad never raised his hand to his grandchildren again, and my husband softened to my father's strictness, but what could have been a happy memory of a rare time together now is a tainted memory of anger and disharmony.

Even in cases where people don't agree with each other, they can recognize and honor differences in opinion. Letting go of being right is not about being passive or becoming a doormat; it's about expressing assertiveness without causing harm.

Letting Go of the Ego

Frequently, the need to be in control takes the form of a need to be right. Some people who have control issues act as if they know what's best for *everyone*, regardless of the situation. Some individuals stop speaking to family members after a disagreement, stubbornly believing their way is the right way and refusing to consider the possibility that they could be wrong. They choose to cut off a family member for behaving differently from how they felt they should behave—they are *right*, the other person is *wrong*, and it's as simple as that. They've made up their mind, and nothing is going to change it. Their anger got them into the fight, and their ego keeps them there—sometimes for the rest of their lives.

Although children are rewarded in school for getting things right, they do not have to be right at *everything*, and most kids still possess the ability to let go of their egos. They will argue with their friends and blurt out things like, "I'm never going to talk to you again!" or "I hate (insert friend's name), and I'm never, ever going to be their friend again!" Then five minutes later, the two kids who were fighting are happily playing together as though nothing ever happened. Children choose to forgive and forget—*they let go of being right.* They jump right back into the friendship with an open mind and an open heart. If only adults were as wise!

As we grow up, our ingrained belief system becomes much more rigid. We find the need to defend our positions and our ways of thinking, sometimes aggressively. In our home lives, our work lives, and even with strangers, we often choose being right over being happy. We spend years and countless hours defending our position, not realizing we're wasting precious time and that putting our need to be right above everything else is isolating and mentally draining.

Our ego works to protect our self-esteem from harm, and we tell ourselves that the other person or group is wrong and that we are right in order to protect the inflated image we have of ourselves. The truth is, most conflicts are rarely black and white. They are often multifaceted, arising from different perspectives and different ways of thinking. Clinging to the belief that our way is the *right* way prevents us from seeing and understanding the other person or group. It creates division rather than resolution.

Families can remain broken because of this stubbornness, and literal wars have been started by leaders who firmly defend their position, believing themselves to always be absolutely right, refusing to listen to anyone who offers another perspective.

In the Middle East and North Africa, women are murdered in "honor killings" because they don't follow rules that the predominantly male-led government imposes. This can manifest in things like choosing to dress a certain way, rebelling against traditional forms of behavior or occupation, or refusing to enter into an arranged marriage. Many times it is the male members of the girl's own family who carry out the honor killings. This is the terrible outcome of some people being so insistent that they are "right."

Although these are horrific, extreme, and severe cases, we can all remember occasions when we have chosen being right over being happy. I know I certainly have, and I regret wasting valuable moments allowing my ego to rule my heart.

Choosing Happiness

Take a moment to think back over your own life. Do you remember times when you prioritized being right over being happy? Perhaps you are still doing it. Have you cut off a family member because you felt that you were right and they were wrong? There are certain times when it is okay to remove a toxic person from your life, and we'll talk more about that later, but for now, think about the wasted moments in your life when you insisted on proving you were right. Think about the anger it caused you or others. Can you imagine a way you could have acted differently?

By choosing to be happy instead of choosing to be right, you will find an enormous amount of freedom. It is a sign of strength, not weakness, to let go of your ego and seek peace instead of conflict. Allowing yourself to let go of control not only increases your happiness and harmony, but it improves your mental health and stress level if you choose to let go of resentment. Alcoholics Anonymous has a well-known saying that applies here: Choosing to hold on to resentment is like drinking poison and expecting the other person to die.

Try this the next time you find yourself immersed in an argument: Before you do anything else, think it through. Although proving you are right may mean "winning," what is it you're actually winning? Ask yourself, *Is this worth losing my friendships, my happiness, and a deeper connection to inner peace?*

Choosing to be happy over being right requires humility, vulnerability, and a willingness to let go of your ego's need for attention and validation. In your relationships, whether personal or professional, insisting on being right may lead to temporary satisfaction but rarely leads to lasting happiness. When we are fixated on our need to be right, we lose sight of the bigger picture, and we begin to erode the common ground that binds us together.

Learning to Really Listen

Sometimes, it's necessary to go back to the basics and relearn some key communication skills like active listening. Practice actually *hearing* the other person and what they are saying instead of formulating your response while they're still speaking. When you listen to understand rather than to win the argument, you will experience more fulfilling interactions. And you may even learn something about other perspectives.

It's okay to embrace humility and admit you don't have all the answers. It's okay to be wrong. It is not a sign of weakness. Being wrong is an opportunity for mental and spiritual growth. As Socrates said, "The man who knows everything learns nothing."

When you choose happiness over "rightness," you prioritize connection, love, and joy. You allow others to hold their own perspectives without feeling threatened by them. You help cultivate inner peace, knowing that being right is not what ultimately defines your self-worth.

There is a lot of freedom in letting things go; it is liberating. It frees you from constantly trying to prove your point; it frees you from the anxiety of being constantly challenged and from the endless cycle of conflict. When you let things go, you open yourself up to a more harmonious and peaceful way of living.

If you really think about it, constantly insisting on being right can hurt those around you. It makes other people feel belittled, dismissed, or unappreciated. Choosing happiness, on the other hand, means valuing the emotions and perspectives of others. Even if you don't agree with them, you can agree to disagree and move on from there.

Practice asking yourself these questions in moments of conflict: *Does this truly matter in the long run? Is it more important to win this argument or to have harmony in this relationship? Will proving my point enhance the situation, or will it push the other person away?* The best way to answer these questions is to have a mindful response. Pause and encourage yourself to be less impulsive. Take a deep breath before responding.

Ask yourself: *Is my response motivated by proving I'm right, or is it aimed at understanding the situation?* Once you answer this question, approach the conversation from a place of openness rather than defensiveness, being mindful of your tone and body language.

Then ask yourself a few more questions: *Why do I feel the need to be right at this moment? Will my comments improve the situation or hinder it? Is it possible that both perspectives hold some truth? Could letting go create more peace for me and the person I'm in conversation with? Could an agreement improve the situation or our relationship?*

You will find freedom in letting go of control and releasing the need to direct the outcome of a situation. This can provide a lot of peace when you accept that not everything can be changed by proving your point. Simply put, it releases the stress of the situation. Like a child who's eager to turn an enemy back into a friend, you can make the choice to let go of resentment, listen to another perspective, and grow wiser and more compassionate as you grow into your best possible self.

11

DON'T LOSE THE LESSON

See Mistakes as Seeds of Opportunity

The secret to winning is
learning how to lose.
—*James Clear*[23]

When my daughter was fourteen years old, I gave her some money to buy a new outfit that she wanted. She was super excited to go shopping in one of her favorite stores with her girlfriends. Before she left, I said to her, as all moms have said at some point to their kids, "Make sure you put your money in a safe place." She spent the afternoon trying on multiple outfits in different parts of the store. But when she finally chose something and it was time to pay, she realized she'd lost the cash I had given her.

She was upset and frantically searched the changing rooms and other areas of the store she'd been in, but sadly, she could not find the money. My daughter confessed to me that the money had been in her pocket when she entered the store, but it wasn't in a very safe place. She assumed that when she was trying on clothes in the changing room and choosing a new outfit, it had most likely fallen out of her pocket. I ended up purchasing the outfit for her but told her, "If you can learn this lesson now, with this amount of money, you will *never* make that mistake again when the stakes may be a lot higher."

Always put money in a safe place. This lesson that my daughter learned when she was a young teen is just a tiny example of learning from our past mistakes, but we all have *many* experiences we can learn from. When life presents a problem that you need to work on or get over, always keep this well-known quote from the Dalai Lama in mind: "When you lose, don't lose the lesson."

The "Never Ever" List

On my phone and on my computer, I have a list titled "Never Ever." It is an ongoing compilation of mistakes I have made in the past that I don't want to repeat. Some of the mistakes are small things like types of nail polish to avoid. Others are big things, like not EVER letting my husband drive in Rome. It consists of things I will never do again . . . *ever*!

The list has had everything on it over the years: names of boyfriends I was totally done with (although I must confess, one or two of them ended up on that list a couple of times), restaurants with terrible food, or beauty salons where I had a particularly bad experience. My current list has Jell-O shots (because they are delicious and I do too many), shots in general, any mystery alcoholic beverage that may have mixed contents, and, more recently, any type of margarita.

I never go on a long drive without first checking the weather and traffic, and I never drive my car on "fumes." I never leave my wallet on my lap when I drive (at least, not after I once lost it this way) or set a cup of coffee next to my seat while driving (ouch!). I never wear improper gear in cold weather or set out on a snowy drive without a warm jacket and shoes I can easily walk in if my car breaks down (been there). I never travel with my most expensive jewelry (added to the list after losing some valuable pieces), and I never forget my phone charger when traveling. I also never trust the box dye highlight kit. It might look appealing in the store when I'm desperate for a color appointment, but it will never look anything like the picture on the box. And on a similar topic, I never cut my own fringe (that's British for bangs). The list goes on. I think you get the message. But all of those things I previously did I learned my lesson the hard way—painful breakups, terrible hangovers, ruined hair and bad experiences in general. If you force yourself to learn from your mistakes, it helps take the sting out of having gone through them.

It's more difficult to learn from the mistakes that are close to your heart. For example, it's hard to learn who someone *really* is after they show you their true colors. Like that friend who only ever calls you when they need something. Or that coworker who continuously lets you down. Or that family member who always takes advantage of you.

Sometimes, life seems to present many lessons to be learned from all at once. These times can feel overwhelming as we go through the pain over and over again: losing a significant amount of money or a sentimental item, getting in a car wreck, navigating a failed relationship, the list goes on. Having a "Never Ever" list, whether mental or physical, of bad experiences that you don't want to repeat or that you no longer want in your life is a valuable practice. It keeps the lessons fresh in your mind and prevents you from repeating your mistakes.

Opportunities in Disguise

Mistakes in life are inevitable, and while they can be uncomfortable and painful, they hold immense value. Every mistake we make carries with it the potential for growth and self-discovery—if we are willing to embrace it. Mistakes can be seeds of opportunity. It is through the lessons we extract from our missteps that we achieve wisdom, resilience, and, ultimately, the strength to forge ahead with greater clarity.

Understanding the importance of learning from mistakes is fundamental to personal development. It transforms setbacks into stepping stones toward success. And sometimes when we feel like our world is falling apart, things are actually falling into place.

Most people fear mistakes, and try to avoid them, because they associate setbacks with failure. However, this mindset limits our potential. In reality, mistakes are simply markers showing us how much we can grow. They indicate that we are trying, that we are exploring, that we are heading into new territory, and that we are pushing our boundaries.

Mistakes can teach us resilience. When we experience failure, we are given the opportunity to reflect on what went wrong and how we can do it differently next time. Resilience is not about avoiding mistakes but recovering from them. It is not how we fall but how we rise. Each time we rise after experiencing a setback, we become stronger and more equipped to face future challenges.

We have all heard the stories about how mistakes sparked innovation and invention. Take, for example, the discovery of penicillin, the invention of Post-it notes, or the invention of the microwave. These breakthroughs all came from accidents, but they became groundbreaking new inventions due to one person's ability to recognize the value in their blunder. When we allow ourselves to experiment, accepting that mistakes are a natural part of the process, we open the door to creativity and innovation.

Embrace Humility

Learning from mistakes requires humility. It's important to acknowledge that we don't have all the answers and that we are sometimes capable of being wrong. This recognition is critical for personal growth. Admitting our shortcomings and taking full responsibility for them allows us to become more in tune with our strengths and our weaknesses, and it highlights the areas where we need self-improvement.

Having the mindset of humility helps us approach life with the feeling of joy that comes from continuous learning. And when something doesn't go as planned, it forces us to reexamine our approach: *What could I have done differently? How could I have made the outcome of the situation better?* By answering these questions truthfully, we uncover new insights that we might have otherwise missed. This simple change in perspective will broaden our understanding of the problem at hand and offer us new solutions and strategies for the future.

Life, as the saying goes, is the greatest teacher. Unlike formal education, where the curriculum is structured and the lessons are neatly organized in textbooks, life presents its lessons in an unpredictable and often chaotic fashion. These lessons come from experience, whether they are moments of joy, sorrow, triumph, or failure, and they are rarely accompanied by explicit instructions or complicated grading systems. What makes life's teachings unique is that they're profoundly personal, constantly evolving, and, if we pay attention to them, capable of fostering resilience, wisdom, and growth.

We're not given a syllabus to life when we're born. We're not told ahead of time when the lessons will come, how they'll be delivered, or what exactly we'll need to learn. One day, you might be on top of the world, and the next, you could face a situation that knocks you to the ground. This unpredictability is part of what makes life challenging, but it's also what makes it enriching. The trick lies in keeping an open mind and having the flexibility to accept what life throws at you, good or bad, and understanding that every experience holds the potential to teach you something valuable.

One of life's most powerful teachers is failure. It's easy to embrace success and bask in the glory of achievement, but failure can feel like a major blow to the ego. However, it's in those moments of downfall, when we are facing rejection or falling short of our goals, where some of life's most important lessons lie. Failure teaches humility and patience. It forces self-reflection, asking us to confront our weaknesses and grow from them.

Michael Jordan, arguably the greatest basketball player of all time, said: "I have missed more than nine thousand shots. I have lost more than three hundred games. Twenty-six times, I have been trusted to take the game's winning shot and missed. I have failed over and over and over in my life. That is why I am so successful."

Think of failure not as an end but as a beginning, as a stepping stone to something greater. Many great inventors, entrepreneurs, artists, and thinkers often speak of their failures as the most valuable parts of their journey. The lessons you learn from getting things wrong are usually more enduring than the fleeting euphoria of immediate success. Take, for example, Thomas Edison, whose thousands of failed experiments led to the invention of the lightbulb. He famously said, "I have not failed. I have just found ten thousand ways that it won't work." Or James Dyson, who went through five thousand prototypes before inventing the first bagless vacuum.

The School of Life

It's an uncomfortable truth that pain is one of the most influential teachers. Whether it's physical or emotional suffering, pain has a way of awakening parts of us that remain dormant during easier times. Pain forces us to slow down, reflect, and reassess what truly matters. When life becomes painful, it's easy to fall into despair or resentment. But if it's approached with patience and wisdom, pain can become a path toward deeper understanding—of yourself, of others, and of the world around you.

Healing from pain teaches empathy and compassion and often leads to a more profound appreciation for life's beauty. The depth of joy you experience is often in direct proportion to the depth of sorrow you've endured. Life is constantly changing, and it demands that we learn the art of adaptability. Nothing in life ever stays the same—circumstances change, people evolve, and situations shift, often without warning. Those who cling too rigidly to the way things are or the way they think things should be are frequently left frustrated and heartbroken.

Adaptability is the ability to bend without breaking, to accept change, and to evolve. It's about understanding that control is often an illusion, and the true power lies in how you respond to the things that are beyond your control. Learning this lesson will give you a sense of peace as you discover how to navigate the currents of your life rather than resist them.

Our relationships can be fertile ground for learning. Whether it's family, friends, colleagues, or romantic partners, each person you interact with becomes a mirror, reflecting parts of yourself. In relationships, you learn about your own strengths, weaknesses, values, and boundaries. Feeling anger can reveal where your boundaries have been crossed—or where you need to set clearer ones. The times when we feel triggered by a person can signal unhealed emotional wounds or unresolved past experiences. For example, if you are triggered by a partner always being late, looking deeper, it may remind you of childhood feelings of abandonment. If you always expect people to immediately respond to your texts and feel anger if they don't, it reflects your assumption that others should always meet your expectations and standards of responsiveness. Relationships bring many lessons if we are willing to look at them objectively.

Life's lessons are not only about what we've experienced in the past or what we hope to achieve in the future; they're also about learning to live in the present moment. Discovering how to be fully present is one of life's most challenging lessons, but also one of the most rewarding. Learning to focus on the *now*, to engage fully with the moment in front of you, is where real contentment lies.

To truly benefit from our mistakes, we must engage in the process of reflection and learning. Here are some ways to do this:

- Acknowledge that you have made a mistake, take full ownership of it, and embrace the situation with the mindset of learning from it.
- Once you've accepted the mistake, analyze what went wrong. Was it due to a lack of preparation, poor decision-making, circumstances beyond your control, or something else?
- Every mistake is a seed of opportunity; it has a lesson embedded in it, but it is up to us to find the lesson. What did going through this experience teach you about yourself and your decisions or the situation you found yourself in? Do you need to learn to communicate better, manage your time better, or approach the problem from a completely different angle?
- Learning from your mistakes is only valuable if you use the knowledge to make meaningful changes. Take action to ensure you don't repeat it. Consider making a list of your mistakes in the notes app on your phone (like my "Never Ever" list).
- Once you've sufficiently analyzed and learned from your mistake, it's time to move on. Don't dwell on the past. Don't let this experience hold you back or prevent you from learning in the future. Use it as a foundation for growth and move forward with a greater sense of purpose and understanding.

Learning from mistakes allows us to be the very best versions of ourselves. It is through this process that we become capable of transforming our setbacks into successes. Allow yourself to no longer fear your mistakes but to see them as tools for lifelong learning and powerful teachers.

If you fail a test because you crammed everything the night before, realize that you retain more by spreading your studying out over days and resolve to make a better study schedule next time.

If you get injured during an intense workout because you haven't exercised in months yet wanted to join the latest workout trend, embrace the importance of gradually easing your way into fitness.

If you bomb a job interview because you were ill-prepared, resolve to learn more about the company you are applying to in your next interview.

If you lash out during an argument or gossip about a friend and damage trust, realize that you need to pause before responding when you're engaged in a heated discussion—and that you need to respect the secrets of your friends.

Life's lessons are deeply personal because they contribute to one's ongoing journey of self-discovery. The more experiences you accumulate, the more you learn about who you *really* are, what you stand for, and what kind of life you want to lead. Self-discovery is not a destination but a continuous lifelong learning process, one that's shaped by every moment, every mistake, every achievement, and every encounter along the way.

Life doesn't hand out grades, but if you learn to pay attention, reflect, and grow, you can create your own measure of success, a life that is authentic to you and has shaped who you are. Choose to see every day as an opportunity to learn, to grow, and to become more of who you're meant to be. The key is to remain open to the lessons that come, embracing them fully with all the joy and all the pain they may bring, and to trust that each experience is shaping you into a wiser, more compassionate, more resilient version of yourself.

12

WEALTH AND MONEY

Realize the Richness of Abundance

Wealth consists not in having great possessions, but in having few wants.

—*Epictetus*

Most of the problems in our world stem from one insatiable human impulse: the desire for *more.* People are driven to want more money, more stuff, more sex, more land, more power. *Bigger! Better! More, more, more!* The idea of the American dream has long stood as a beacon of hope and aspiration, a concept that promised equality, freedom, and opportunity for all. It was the belief that with hard work and determination, anyone, regardless of their background, could achieve a better life. Over time, however, the American dream morphed from a noble aspiration to something more elusive and distorted, driven by consumerism and a relentless and often insatiable quest for more.

According to an article from encyclopedia.com, the concept of the American dream has its roots in the founding principles of the United States.[24] The early Puritans believed that their hard work and faithfulness to God would result in a "city upon a hill," a society blessed with prosperity and moral virtue. As the country expanded, waves of immigrants arrived, drawn by the belief that America offered the opportunity to escape oppression and hardship, promising a new life where success was attainable.

Throughout the mid-twentieth century, the American dream was primarily characterized by economic stability and upward mobility. The post–World War II era, particularly the 1950s, is often viewed as the golden age of the American dream. For certain segments of society—notably white, educated males—the economy was booming, unemployment was low, and home ownership was rising. A typical depiction of the American dream during this period was a middle-class family living in a suburban home with a steady job and access to education and healthcare. But, like most things, that image was too good to be true.

The American Nightmare

As the American economy continued to grow in the latter half of the twentieth century, the American dream became less about achieving security and more about acquiring symbols of success—brand-new cars, luxury homes, fashionable designer clothing, and the latest technology and gadgets. These items became not just products to purchase but symbols of status and fulfillment. The rise of television during this era made mass marketing more effective as corporations learned to appeal to the desires and fantasies of the American public.

By the 1980s, this shift had reached new heights. During this period, the notion of "greed is good," epitomized by the character Gordon Gekko in the movie *Wall Street*, became a cultural touchstone. Success was increasingly measured not by stability and security but by displays of material wealth. The American dream, once a vision of modest prosperity and fairness, began to transform into a culture of excess. Corporations encouraged Americans to buy bigger, buy better, buy newer, and buy more. Credit, particularly in the form of credit cards, became more readily available, allowing people to live far beyond their means further feeding the frenzy of a consumption-driven society.

In the twenty-first century, the rise of digital technology, particularly the advent of social media and reality television, further transformed the American dream. Platforms like Instagram, Facebook, TikTok, and X (Twitter) have made it easier than ever to compare oneself to others. This constant exposure to the carefully curated lives of celebrities and "influencers," including the world's most wealthy and successful, has intensified feelings of inadequacy and the desire for *more* still.

In a world where influencers flaunt luxury lifestyles and billionaires like Jeff Bezos and Elon Musk dominate the news, the gap between aspiration and reality has widened. The dream of simply having a comfortable life has, for many, been replaced by the pursuit of wealth and fame, often at the expense of personal well-being as was so often depicted on the Bravo network's reality shows, where so many cast members lived well *beyond* their means—and were celebrated for it.

This has given rise to "hustle culture" where people are encouraged to work tirelessly, always seeking the next big thing, the next promotion, or the next income stream. This relentless pursuit has led to extreme burnout, personal dissatisfaction, and even a mental health crisis, where too much is never enough.

In so many ways, the digital age has turned the American dream into a nightmare where the pursuit of *more* is never-ending. The idea of contentment has become elusive, replaced by the insatiable desire for more wealth, more recognition, and more prestige, and it is far worse in America than in the whole of Europe combined.

Socially, it has exacerbated divisions, as those left behind by economic changes feel increasingly disenfranchised. As the saying goes, the rich get richer and the poor get poorer. Economic inequality has deepened, leading to political polarization and a sense of disillusionment.

The desire for *more* has driven overconsumption, resource depletion, and the degradation of our forests and ecosystems. The pursuit of endless economic growth, fueled by consumer demand, has come at a very high cost to the planet with waste that is accumulated each year from things we once wanted but no longer have the desire for: clothes, shoes, makeup, gadgets, home decor, dorm furnishings, cars, yard furniture, kids' toys, and more. Where do all of these things end up when we are done with them? In landfills, which tell the sad story of decades of discarding without any thought as to what this may be doing to our environment.

The American dream has changed, but it still persists. The challenge moving forward will be to reclaim it from the forces of greed and overconsumption and to redefine it in a way that reflects the actual needs and values of our modern, diverse society.

Never Enough

My mother, who raised us on a modest income, would always remind me, "You're only poor when you want more than you have." Despite her relative poverty, she lived richly, appreciating what she had instead of constantly chasing what she didn't. Her wisdom influenced me, but not until later in my life. For many years, I found myself caught in the grip of *wanting more*. Because I'd grown up feeling "poor," money became an obsession for me. I falsely believed that financial security was the key to escaping my feelings of lack and being less than.

I worked tirelessly, taking on multiple jobs at once, to reach arbitrary financial milestones. In my twenties, I had a goal to save one hundred thousand dollars, and yet the moment I achieved that goal, I wanted even more. I thought having more money would make me feel safe, but the truth was that no amount of wealth would ever ease the underlying fear that I didn't have enough. I was caught up in the cycle of working and saving, followed by even more working and saving, in order to "build my financial backbone."

Eventually, I realized that my fixation on money was rooted in insecurity. It had nothing to do with how much I had and everything to do with how I felt about myself. I have seen this same pattern in many people I've met even in billionaires. Some of the wealthiest people I know live a very humble and modest life, afraid to spend any of their money—even on others. They only care about their growing bank balances. I've met very wealthy people who are miserable and have lived (and died) forever chasing more. These people have *everything*—big houses, private jets, many successful businesses, the best of everything—but their desire for *more* dominates their lives. They never found true happiness or satisfaction and were blind to the fact that they could lose everything they'd worked for with one wrong decision or legal misstep. And for some, the pursuit of *more* has led to ruin—financially and personally.

There's a deep irony in the way we chase after money, thinking that having more of it will solve our problems. The reality is that money, when pursued endlessly, can create more problems than it solves. The more businesses you acquire and the more homes you have, the more responsibilities, stressors, and potential problems you have. When we're driven by the need for *more*, we enter a cycle of dissatisfaction. We think, *If only I had a bigger house, a better car, and more financial security, then I'd be happy.* But the moment we achieve those things, the goalpost shifts. Suddenly, the house isn't big enough, the car is outdated, the designer bag is out of style, and we need even more money for the next even bigger thing.

I've seen this play out in people's lives repeatedly, including my own. There's always bigger, always someone just ahead of us. The tragedy is that while people are busy accumulating wealth, they often miss out on the experiences that bring true fulfillment, like spending time with loved ones, working on their own personal growth, and experiencing the joy of simple pleasures. One of the hardest financial skills for a wealthy person to learn is knowing when they have *enough*. A 2010 study by Nobel Prize-winners Daniel Kahneman and Angus Deaton showed that happiness can only be increased by money up to a certain point, which is about $75,000 per year.

The obsession with *more* can also isolate us from others. In the pursuit of wealth, relationships can be sacrificed. We see friends as competition, not companions. We work longer hours, missing family dinners, children's milestones, outings with friends, and moments that truly matter. By the time we realize what we've lost, it's often much too late to recover those connections.

One of the most common myths surrounding money is the idea that financial security will protect us from life's uncertainties. We tell ourselves that if we save enough, invest wisely, or accumulate substantial wealth, we'll be immune to hardship. But money cannot shield us from many things, including heartache, loneliness, disease, mental illness, the loss of loved ones, or the existential crises we all face at some point.

No amount of money can buy back time or undo a loss of a loved one. The pursuit of financial security can, in fact, blind us to the reality that true security comes from within, from knowing who we are, from trusting that we can handle whatever life throws at us. Although this may be hard to understand, it's a paradox: The more you try to secure yourself with wealth, the more fragile you often feel.

Living Richly

If we look at wealth through a different lens, we begin to see that the things that make life truly rich aren't tied to our bank accounts. Real wealth is found in moments of connection, in being present for the people we love, in having the freedom to pursue our passions, in experiencing the world with a sense of joy, curiosity, and wonder. True wealth is the peace of mind that comes from knowing you are enough just as you are, without needing external validation from the things you own. It's the strength to walk through life with resilience, finding joy in the journey rather than constantly reaching for the next material goal.

Warren Buffett is worth over $142 *billion*. Yet he drives an average car, and he's lived in the same house he bought sixty years ago. For him, wealth isn't about flaunting how much you're worth—it's about holding on to the money you earn. He earned money from his stocks, and he protected his profit. He has not wasted his money on material possessions but has donated millions to causes close to his heart, to benefit the lives of others.

You can also be rich without having a ton of money in the bank or an impressive stock portfolio. For my mother, wealth meant investing in relationships, dedicating herself to personal growth, and creating a life filled with meaning. Now I'm learning the same lesson she modeled—that the best returns come not from financial investments but from the investments we make in ourselves and others. It's the love we give and receive, the joy we spread, and the lives we touch that show us just how rich we really are.

In the end, money is just a tool. Yes, it can bring comfort and security, but it should never be the only goal of life. Yes, we should work hard and save sensibly for the future, but we should be careful not to turn money into an idol. Instead of asking, "How much money do I need to be happy?" we should ask, "How can I use the resources I have to build a life that feels meaningful?" That shift in mindset changes everything. We stop measuring success by the size of our bank accounts and start measuring it by the quality of our lives. What truly matters isn't how much we've accumulated but how fully we've lived.

Stealing Is Never Free

I've had many things stolen from me, both material and emotional. Those losses were often painful and left scars that took time to heal. It's hard not to feel bitterness when someone rips away something you've worked so hard for. But as difficult as it was, I realized over time that what helped me the most in those situations was not clinging to bitterness but instead understanding the more profound spiritual laws at play—specifically, that thieves eventually get what is coming to them.

Regardless of your belief system, whether you're religious, spiritual, or just philosophical, certain truths seem universal: *You reap what you sow. What goes around comes around. Karma is getting what you deserve and deserving what you get.* Every culture and every tradition seems to have some version of this concept. When someone steals something, they might walk away with an item of value in that moment, but they *will* lose something, and it's almost always far more precious than the thing they stole.

I've seen it happen many times in my own life and in the lives of others: Dishonesty always bites back, often with interest. This is why I urge anyone who might be tempted to steal or cheat—just don't. Even if the law never catches up with you, or you *think* nobody will ever find out, there will always be a price to pay eventually.

When you steal, it sends a message to the Universe that you're operating from a place of scarcity, that you don't believe there is enough for you. This creates a cycle of lack, perpetuating feelings of never having enough. This is the message you are sending out: *I don't have enough, I am lacking, and I need to break moral and societal codes to get* more *because I am unworthy and cannot do it the right way.*

You will *always* have to pay it back—often with a lot of interest. It may not be the item that you stole (obviously), but it could be something more costly for you.

When I think about the men who robbed me in the nail salon (or any other thief), I actually feel sorry for those criminals. They may have gotten a few hundred dollars, or even tens of thousands of dollars, a car, jewelry, or something else, but those items are worthless and useless in the grand scheme of life. They may have enjoyed what they stole for a while, but soon after, they faced the payback of having to live the rest of their lives behind bars.

Living in Abundance

Cheating or stealing means you are not living from a place of abundance. With abundance, you would never consider those actions because you trust that life will provide you with all you need to live well and be happy. This is the message you are putting out to the Universe. When you live with a mindset of abundance, you are able to break free from the cycle of lack. When you trust that there is enough for you and everyone else in the world, you stop living in fear, and you stop looking to take what isn't already yours. You are able to live a free and happy life with what you have.

I encourage everyone to begin what may be a new practice: saying a prayer for abundance. I say one that is personal to me; you can use my prayer, but you might want to change its words so it's more personal to you. Recite the prayer each day to begin to live from a place of abundance, and don't allow your past thoughts and experiences to keep you in the feeling of lack.

The more you live from a place of abundance, the more gifts will come into your life. Remember, this is not for excess or to be greedy but for the good of all. With an abundant mindset, you welcome collaboration and differing perspectives, and you don't see others as competition or a threat. You believe that there is more than enough opportunity, so you are generous with your time and ideas. Your openness and trust in abundance sets a positive cycle in motion. The people you meet and share ideas with will give back to you if you work with like-minded individuals.

When you believe that there is enough success, love, and resources to go around, you act generously rather than fearfully, and that energy tends to come back to you. You will have moments of synchronicity where you feel that you are being given gifts from the Universe. And that, I promise, will always be enough.

A PRAYER FOR ABUNDANCE

This is a nondenominational prayer, but feel free to change the words to fit with your spiritual beliefs.

Dear Source of All Blessings:

I come to you with a grateful and trusting heart. I thank you for my many blessings, and I ask that you keep them coming. Thank you for your infinite generosity and goodness. Thank you for blessing me with abundance, health, wealth, and prosperity. Thank you for filling my life with love, joy, and peace. I ask that my opportunities grow and prosper so that I may use my gifts for good. I ask that the abundance flows to me and through me, so that I may bring love and light to others. Help me to remain humble and mindful, appreciating each of my blessings, and may my heart be open to receiving them. Thank you for the abundance already present in my life and for the unlimited blessings yet to come. Amen.

13

RELATIONSHIPS

Perfect the Art of Letting Go

A healthy relationship is a feast of affection and giving for both people, not one person receiving crumbs and trying to convince themselves it's enough.
—*Shannon Thomas*

At the time of writing this book, I have been married twenty-two years and with my husband for twenty-three. I never thought I was the kind of person who would be able to make a marriage last so long. Before I got married, my biological clock was ticking like a time bomb. I had hit thirty with a failed long-term relationship in my rearview mirror and no potential suitors on the horizon. I was worried that I was destined to be childless and alone, or that I'd get stuck in the kind of relationship where I needed to make a lot of compromises in order to be happy. Then I met my now husband.

Before marriage, I naively believed that marriage was the goal. But once I got married, I realized it's just the beginning. Any problems you have *before* you get married will only be magnified afterwards, and once you add kids to the equation, all hell breaks loose. Luckily, my husband and I did not bring much unknown baggage into our marriage, because we'd gotten to know each other as friends first and been very open, telling each other pretty much everything about ourselves. But once we had kids, we discovered that we had different ideas about how we should raise our children.

My husband was brought up with a lot more privilege than I'd experienced. He was raised with nannies, maids, and drivers, extravagant European vacations, and enough money to make most problems go away. I had been raised by a hardworking mum and dad who had just enough money to give their children a good upbringing but did most everything for themselves. Therefore we had no nannies, maids, or drivers, just my hands on mum. This was the first hurdle my husband and I had to face in our marriage. He wanted a live-in nanny, and I wanted to be a hands-on mom. We eventually settled for wonderful daytime nannies so that I could return to work and a full-time nanny after our second child was born. I had two kids under two and little time for myself. Still, this topic and some other financial arguments went on for about the first ten years of our kids' lives. I wanted our daughter and son to know the value of a dollar, and my husband wanted to give them everything and want for nothing. I am happy to say that despite their parents' differences, our kids turned out to be hardworking, independent individuals who definitely know the value of a dollar. But I learned the lesson that that every relationship is a series of compromises, and a marriage is decades of that if you have a good one.

A Mother's Happiness

As any parent knows, if your child is suffering, then the parent is also suffering, because since their birth, our main goal has been the well-being of our kids. A mother's primary DNA is to raise and take care of her offspring and help them thrive, maintaining their survival, and, therefore, the survival of the planet. This works due to a combination of biological, emotional, and social factors, evolution, and the mother's instinct to protect her offspring. From a biological perspective, oxytocin, sometimes called the "bonding" or "love" hormone, strengthens the emotional connection between a mother and her child, reinforcing these protective behaviors.

Most mothers feel a deep sense of responsibility and attachment, driven by empathy, love, and a desire to provide a secure environment for their children. Mothers are often a young child's primary caregiver, and their job is to safeguard their child from harm so they can grow and thrive in their most vulnerable years. As children grow older, leave the nest, and begin to fend for themselves, we learn to detach and let them go freely into the world, hoping that our job as parents has been sufficient to give them what they need to thrive as young adults. But it's not as if we completely let go. A mother's happiness can be permanently tied to the happiness of her children. This is the way it is for me and most of the mothers I know. (Fathers, too, but I'm a mom, so mothering is what I know.)

Recently, I've been contemplating the idea that "a mother is only as happy as her least happy child." For quite some time now, this phrase has been running through my head like a distorted 45 vinyl disc, playing on a loudspeaker, coming and going like a self-help mantra in reverse.

The year I was assaulted in the nail salon was a challenging year for our family. After that terrifying experience, I felt like I couldn't live in Atlanta anymore; I was severely traumatized and no longer felt safe in my home or the surrounding neighborhoods. I would spend an unhealthy amount of time dwelling on my exit and survival plan, should I be attacked again. Every time I went to the grocery store, cinema, school, church, or mall, I would be thinking through an exit strategy in case a gunman opened fire. I was consumed by the fear of it happening again, suffering from PTSD, and that's no way to live. Eventually, we sold our home; my husband sold his medical practice, and we moved out of state to set up a new life for ourselves in Aspen, Colorado.

Living in Aspen was nothing new for me. I had lived there for twelve years. In fact, when I first met my husband, I was living in Aspen, but it made sense for us to begin our married lives together in Atlanta so my husband didn't have to restart his medical practice in Colorado. So I sold my home, along with the film production company I owned, left behind family and friends, and moved across the country. The plan was to move back to Colorado in five years, but five years became ten, and then ten years became twenty.

Now here I was, twenty years later, moving back to Colorado, packing up my entire life and (once again) moving out of state—basically, doing what I'd done twenty years ago, only in reverse. I was both excited and nervous all at the same time. I knew I would love living near my only remaining sister and lifelong best friend, her beautiful family, and many of my old friends, but I worried for our children. After all, Atlanta was the only place they'd ever known.

My husband was thrilled. He sold his medical practice, excited to take early retirement and join some medical missions. Our daughter had just started college, so she, too, had a new path ahead of her, getting settled into life on campus and adjusting to living in a new state.

Our son, on the other hand, was *devastated.* He was in his junior year of high school and didn't want to leave his friends and the city he loved. For the first month of our new life in Colorado, we did everything we could to try to make him happy. We set him up in the caretaker's apartment, which was connected to our house, and gave him a car, a generous allowance, and a lot more freedom than he'd ever had in Atlanta. As the weeks passed and his mood didn't improve, I began to think we'd made a colossal mistake moving back to Colorado. I felt extremely guilty that we had put him through this for his junior year of high school, and worried about his mood changes and behavior, I enlisted a local therapist to help him navigate his new situation, giving him an outlet to vent about how angry he was that he'd had to leave everything that he'd ever known behind.

Despite seeing a therapist, nothing changed. My son was still angry, and it was putting a strain on his relationship with my husband and me. I began to lose sleep over the situation. This new dream life we'd set up for ourselves wasn't turning out like we'd planned. My husband and I argued daily about which course of action we should take regarding our son. We had entirely different viewpoints, and we could not see eye to eye about the situation. Besides not being able to sleep, I began to lose my natural enthusiasm for the things I'd once loved. I was no stranger to depression, and I realized it was time to once again do the work of getting myself into a better place.

Doing "The Work"

When you have suffered with mental health issues as long as I have, you learn what works and what doesn't. So luckily, when the sh*t hits the fan, as it so often does, you have tricks in your pocket you can pull out to help you get through the difficult times. I returned to the teachings of those who had inspired me the most over the years: Deepak Chopra, Byron Katie, Dr. Wayne Dyer. *What would they do in a situation like this?* I asked myself.

In order to rescue myself from my melancholy and help alleviate the stress this situation was causing me, I imagined myself sitting across from Byron Katie in one of her live seminars. Byron has coached thousands of people on relationship issues and often asks the question, "Who is suffering?" I thought about this for a moment, and then replied, "Well, my son is suffering."

"Right, your son is suffering," she said. "And where are you right now?"

"Well, I'm sitting here in my kitchen, drinking a cup of coffee."

"Okay," she responded, "Tell me about that."

"Well, I'm sitting here in my kitchen, drinking a cup of delicious coffee. The sun is shining in through the window, and outside, I can see my dog playing in the grass. I am safe in my home, I am healthy, I am not hurt, and there is nothing bad happening."

"Okay, so what stories are you telling yourself?" was Byron's next gentle prompt.

What was causing me the most pain was the stories I was telling myself about my son and how much he was suffering. I spent most of my day worrying about him, scared that he would never feel any better. I found it extremely hard to detach from these feelings, but I knew I needed to work on this every day.

When you're in the midst of difficult times, it often helps if you make up a personal mantra. One of my favorites that is quick and easy to say is: "Into the open hand, falls freedom." I first read this quote in the book *Journey to Center* by aikido master Thomas Crum.[25] It reminded me to not clutch too tightly to the outcome of any situation, but to instead let things flow and allow the Universe to take control. This is often when the magic happens. We may be focused on one particular outcome, when the Universe has something much bigger or better in mind. So I focused on writing down all the things I want to release. I wanted to let go of feeling responsible for my son's happiness, to let go of my fear that maybe he would never adjust to this new life. I tried to let go of my attachment to any given outcome for me or for him, and I asked God and the Universe to take control of the situation. Some people like to do this act of letting go in a firepit ceremony, where they write down everything they want to release on a piece of paper and then burn, it symbolically letting go. Others prefer to bury the paper in the ground, allowing their worries to be released into the Universe as the paper disintegrates. When I was finally able to let go of the worries I had about my son, things began to change. He met some great friends at his high school, fell in love with a beautiful girl, and after he graduated from high school and had started packing for college, he expressed that he was actually sad to be leaving his life in Aspen. Who would have thought? It turns out the suffering I was doing on his behalf wasn't helping anyone; it was only hurting me. My son had just needed more time to transition through this change, and more space to find his way.

Empty Nest

Many parents feel lost when their children leave home. This is especially true when the last eighteen-plus years of your life have been devoted to doing absolutely everything for those little ones, who have often been the center of your existence. All of a sudden, they are gone, off to college or a job away from home, and on their way to autonomy. Parents are left with an empty home and sadness in their hearts. We miss the days of kids noisily running around the house and the hustle and bustle of school and activities. While it can be hard to let go, it is one of the best gifts we can give our children—letting go teaches them that we trust them to handle life on their own. We may be tempted to step in and save them, to prevent them from failing. But standing back and letting them do things their own way, even if that means failing, is crucial for their development and self-esteem.

Learning and practicing detachment is necessary for our own mental and spiritual health too. It was hard for me to let my kids go, as any parent will understand, because we want everything to be okay for our children and we want to protect them when they go out into the world. But it's so important to *let go*. To trust them and to trust that they will be ok as they navigate the world. For this I always find strength in Deepak Chopra's concept, the law of detachment from his book *The Seven Spiritual Laws of Success*, which I read many decades ago. Back then, I highlighted each chapter, thinking of the book as my guide to life. I still have my original copy, the worn pages falling out of the binding, and although the highlighting is somewhat faded, the words still remain so true. This book contains one of the most beneficial teachings I've ever come across, a teaching that is as simple as it is profound: *Detachment is the letting go of our rigid attachment to the outcome of our situations and desires.*[26]

Chopra explains that while it is essential to set goals, clinging to a particular outcome only creates *resistance* and *anxiety*, blocking the universal flow of all possibilities. He encourages readers to embrace uncertainty, rather than trying to control how things unfold, and to detach from their thoughts about how things should manifest. By trusting the Universe and letting go of control, you find *freedom*. You can trust the process and allow things to fall naturally into place. It is a concept I have tried to live by for most of my adult life, and it has helped me immensely, both mentally and spiritually, on so many occasions. It certainly helped me when my kids left home, but it can be applied to any situation that requires letting go.

The Only Person You Can Change Is You

The reality is, we cannot control most situations, nor can we control the other people in our lives. We will only find resistance from the person we are trying to control. As a teenager and young adult, I used to get quite angry when I couldn't control events, the way things worked out, or the actions of others. I blindly believed I actually had some control over another person or event, and I would do everything I could to make things work out the way I wanted them to. But the more I tried to control things, the more resistance I encountered—and the angrier I would get. Now I understand that I have little control over how things turn out or the actions of another individual. The only person I can change is myself, and by giving up my attachment to the behaviors of others, it allows me to free up my energy to focus on my own actions.

The main thing we must let go of is our *ego*. The ego mind will always try to control everything in order to validate itself. Trusting in yourself, even when you don't know how things will work out, is a powerful way to let the Universe know you are ready to receive and are open to its magic. And those who believe in this magic will always find it. But in order to do this, we need to find our peace in the present moment instead of worrying about the future or dwelling on the past. By engaging in the *now*, we find a great sense of peace and acceptance.

REFLECTION: LETTING GO IN RELATIONSHIPS

Whether it's someone you are dating, a fiancé, a spouse, a parent, a child, a coworker, or a neighbor, relationships can bring both happiness and misery at the same time. Take a moment to think about the relationships in your life and ask yourself the following questions:

- *What relationships are causing me pain?*
- *What is the pain I am hanging on to?*
- *What am I trying to change about the other person?*
- *Is there something I could let go of?*
- *Is there something I could give up to the Universe?*

- *Can I release my grip and open my mind to allow freedom to fall into it so I am no longer holding on so tightly?*
- *How could I change so that I am not affected by the person or situation?*

Take a moment to ponder these questions and then write down five things you could do to feel better about and less controlled by this relationship.

Setting Boundaries in Codependent and Other Unhealthy Relationships

If you are in a relationship with a person who manipulates, lies to, or gaslights you, it is often difficult to think clearly. You often find yourself caught up in a whirlwind of mixed emotions. Your heart knows that something is wrong, and you feel it in your gut, but the other person's words mislead you so much that you find incongruence between your head and your heart. As you travel this bewildering path, each conversation and interaction becomes a challenge to navigate. You may find yourself walking on eggshells to please them. If this all sounds familiar, welcome to club co-dependency.

Codependency is a circular relationship in which one person needs the other person, who, in turn, needs to be needed. The codependent person, known as the "giver," feels worthless unless they are needed by and making sacrifices for the enabler, otherwise known as the "taker." In codependent relationships, people will often display some of the following traits:

- Having an exaggerated sense of responsibility for the actions of others
- Confusing love and pity, with a tendency to "love" people they can pity and rescue
- Doing more than their share in the relationship
- Clinging to an unhealthy dependence on relationships, doing anything to avoid abandonment
- Showing an extreme need for approval and recognition
- Expressing guilt when asserting themselves
- Having a compelling need to control others
- Lacking trust in themselves and/or others
- Fearing being abandoned or alone
- Having difficulty identifying their own feelings
- Feeling rigid and struggling to adjust to change
- Demonstrating problems with intimacy or personal boundaries
- Feeling chronic anger and resorting to lying or dishonesty

Leaving a relationship that is unhealthy or setting up protective boundaries can be extremely difficult, especially if you have become deeply immersed in the day-to-day dynamics of the relationship. You may fail to see its slow demise and how it has been negatively changing you. Friends may try to help you or give you advice, but you don't listen to them, unable to see the reality of the situation you're in. Perhaps you are hanging on to the hope that one day things will magically change. If this sounds familiar, you may need to bring in outside help so you can find the courage to put some healthy boundaries in place.

I always tell my children that people will treat you the way you *teach* them to treat you. If you set up boundaries early on in a relationship, those boundaries will remain in place, but if you allow another person to treat you poorly or disrespect you—and you continue to allow that—then it's much harder to set those boundaries later. Only you can put these limits in place, and the sooner you do it, the better. Be firm about the things you will *not* tolerate in any type of relationship, whether it's with a friend, a coworker, or a significant other.

For me, lying, cheating, or abusing substances (such as alcohol or drugs) is a firm NO. It is impossible for me to have an intimate relationship with someone who is not being honest with me. Unfortunately, I've been down that road before in a past relationship, and I suffered immensely. After that experience, I decided I wasn't going to get involved with—and especially marry—anyone with those tendencies. When I got to know the man who eventually became my husband, I knew he wasn't going to behave in that way, and that was one of the reasons I decided to marry him.

I also have a list of boundaries I put in place for friendships. I don't waste my time with people who are closed-minded, bigoted, or speak badly about others. In my female friendships, I choose to be friends with women who support other women and lift them up. I don't spend much time with people who are not compassionate to immigrants, minorities, or anyone in the LGBTQ community. These things are very personal for me, but everyone must make their own list.

Creating healthy boundaries helps you understand what kind of treatment you will accept from your relationships. By having an idea of what is healthy for your mental and spiritual well-being, you will no longer attract the kind of people who don't align with who you are and who you want to be.

True Intimacy

People often equate intimacy with sexual relationships, but in reality, an intimate relationship is so much more than physical. True intimacy is a bond; it's about the sharing of your true, authentic self—your *real* self—with another human. There are many people in long-term sexual relationships that lack intimacy. That's because intimacy is something *much deeper* than just the physical bond. Intimacy is sharing the parts of yourself that you may not love, the parts that you normally try to hide.

True intimacy is about allowing another person to love and accept you just the way you are. It is a deep connection in which you know you are loved unconditionally. By sharing your fears and insecurities, your pain, and your trauma with a person who doesn't judge you but listens to you and shows you kindness and love, you allow yourself a secure space to heal and grow stronger. In an intimate relationship, you should feel heard, protected, and safe—not anxious and like you're being judged. That is *true* intimacy, and it can be a rare thing for many people to experience. So if you find this with another human, hang on to it and cherish it.

INTIMACY PRINCIPLES AND DEFINITIONS

As you venture into new relationships or reflect on existing ones, keep these intimacy principles and definitions in mind:

- **Boundaries:** Setting clear boundaries protects your mental and spiritual well-being, ensuring healthy, respectful interactions. Set clear and consistent boundaries early in your relationships so that the other person knows what you will and will **not** stand for. If those boundaries are constantly disrespected, then maybe it's time to walk away.
- **Codependency:** Codependent relationships are unhealthy, marked by an imbalance of sacrifice and need; boundaries and balance are essential for healthy relationships.
- **Control and Ego:** The only person we can change is ourselves; we can't change the actions or behaviors of others. Don't waste your time and energy trying to change another person.
- **Detachment:** Let go of rigid attachment to outcomes. Trust the Universe! This will relieve stress and facilitate peace.

- **Letting Go in Relationships:** Reflect on any painful relationships. Focus on what you learned from that experience and make the decision not to repeat it.
- **Self-Intimacy:** Experiencing true intimacy with yourself is key. Do you feel safe in your own company? Do you love yourself unconditionally? Do you pick on yourself? Remember to be kind to yourself—first and foremost, be your own best friend.
- **True Intimacy:** True intimacy is about emotional connection and unconditional love, not just physical attraction—it's rare and invaluable. If you have it, cherish it.

14

FORGIVENESS

Free Yourself from a Lifetime of Pain

Choosing not to forgive is like paying
interest on a loan; you are paying more
for something that has already hurt you,
something that has already happened.
—*Kari Wells*

In the journey of life, forgiveness is the key that will unlock the door to true mental and spiritual well-being, opening yourself up to boundless possibilities. Forgiving others is essential for spiritual growth because thoughts of resentment, anger, and hatred represent slow, debilitating energies that will disempower you if you continue to let them occupy space in your head. If you can release them, you will find peace. How empowering to realize that the experience of being hurt by someone, while painful, is nothing more than a thought or feeling you carry around!

One of the hardest things I've ever had to learn, and one of the things I've struggled with the most, is *letting things go*. Like many of you, there have been times in my life where I felt I had been wronged. Maybe somebody has lied to you, gaslit you, or still blames you for something they did wrong. Perhaps you have a complicated relationship with a family member whom you find hard to forgive. When these things happen, it is hard to let go and forgive. But if you want to have peace in your life, it's the first thing you must do.

Forgiving, Especially When It's Hard

The longer you hold on to pain, the higher the price you pay. The harm has already been done, and you are adding to the pain by choosing to allow the hurt to still anger you.

I genuinely believe the amount you can forgive is proportional to the amount of happiness in your life. I realize that forgiving someone is not easy to do, but believe me, it's powerful. As you can imagine, it was incredibly hard for me to fully forgive the men who had robbed and beaten me, or our former employee who stole from us. I awoke one morning after the assault with this feeling weighing heavy on my heart. I knew it was time for me to let it go. I often take the time to meditate when faced with a difficult task or situation, and then, after my meditation, I discover a solution. So I spent some time meditating on this situation.

I sent a blessing to each of the people who had hurt me. I imagined each of them as a hurt child, lashing out in their pain, not having the emotional intelligence to know the right thing to do. By doing this, I was able to find it easier to understand them and, in turn, to forgive them.

As I thought about the men who assaulted me, I found myself wondering more about them. What was their life like? How were they raised? Had *they* been abused or beaten as children? What had happened to make them so removed from love or conscience? Had they become broken from their experiences? Or were they just violent sociopaths who hated society?

I pictured them in their prison cells, seeing just bars and concrete walls, living out every day the same way, trapped inside a cell. I imagined myself visiting them. I mentally arranged a visit and went to see them one by one. I brought each of them a gift of a small flower. I picked out a beautiful prayer card for each of them to bless them and show them they were still loved by God and the Universe. I imagined our eyes meeting for the first time since we'd seen each other in court. Even though this meeting was just in my mind, I started to feel the physical sensations of fear in my body—my chest became tight, my pulse raced, and my breathing became quick and heavy. Although I knew these men were not anywhere near me and were unable to hurt me, I still began to feel afraid.

Then, I thought about the teachings of Jesus and other great spiritual leaders who talked about the importance of love and forgiveness. Jesus did not spend his life with the kings and queens of his time; he gave his attention to the sinners, the thieves, the poor, the weak, and the sick. He forgave those whom nobody could forgive. When I thought of this, I was able to mentally smile at the men who had assaulted me and tell them how their actions had affected my life. I expressed to them how hurt I had been, how my brain still felt like it had not fully recovered from my injury, but that I still forgave them. It was hard for me to (mentally) face these men who had hurt me so much and filled me with so much terror, but after I did, I immediately felt the sensation of fear leave my body. Perhaps one day I will go to them in person. I would like them to know that they are *forgiven*. I want them to feel it so that they can show it to others and pay it forward.

Strangely, I found it easier to forgive the men who had robbed and beaten me than our former staff member, whom I'd trusted so much. To discover that she had been lying to and stealing from us was beyond heartbreaking. With the gun-toting robbers, it was nothing personal; they were just out to get some money and rob some people. In that situation, I just happened to be in the wrong place at the wrong time. But our former staff member had been in our lives for twelve years; I knew her family, and she knew mine. We had helped her with financial problems, illnesses, and family tragedies. We had mourned with her when her daughter died. She attended our parties and events, and all that time, she had been deceiving us.

I had to work hard to forgive her. I had to remind myself that forgiveness is *not* for the other person; it is for you. It allows *you* to walk away free from the pain the other person has caused you. After I forgave her, I began to feel genuine sympathy toward her—how messed up her life must have been that she would steal from two hardworking people who had been so good to her and had helped her so much.

Self-Forgiveness

At this point in my life, I believe I have forgiven everyone who ever hurt me. But for a long time, I had a recurring dream that involved an old boyfriend who had cheated on me. This was not any kind of romantic dream, because I no longer had feelings for this guy. Yet, for over two years, I experienced this strange, recurring dream. The details and the events that unfolded in the dream were not always the same, but it always had the same common factor: I always felt worthless, like I didn't quite belong in whatever situation the dream presented. I felt like I didn't deserve to be where I was or that I didn't quite fit in. The sentiment of the dream was always a feeling of lack—my self-worth was low, and I wasn't good enough or special enough to belong in whatever place the dream took me. It was quite startling to dream this, because in my real life, I felt nothing like this.

I struggled for a long time with this perplexing dream. I couldn't understand why I was having dreams about my ex, especially because I was now happily married and deeply in love with my husband. Finally, after some deep contemplation, I realized the person in this dream I needed to forgive was *myself.* I needed to forgive myself for not having enough self-worth and self-esteem at that time to leave my ex when he was being so disrespectful toward me. I needed to forgive myself for not choosing to leave sooner and for putting up with his lies and his B.S. Mostly, I needed to forgive myself for spending all that time with a person who didn't fully appreciate me, for choosing to give my heart to someone who didn't deserve it. Once I realized this, I took the time to apologize to my former self. And from that day forward, I never had the dream again.

Remember, forgiveness is for no one else but *you*, so give yourself that gift. You are the one who will heal when you decide to let things go and forgive. By deciding to move forward, you will reap many mental health benefits and feel less burdened in your day-to-day life. Forgiveness frees your soul. It takes away the anger that burns inside of you. It brings you peace and promotes emotional well-being. It allows you to process emotions rather than suppress them, leading to greater emotional resilience. Holding on to grudges increases your stress levels. Forgiveness helps you alleviate this burden, leading to a calmer mind. Letting go of anger and resentment will enhance your overall mood and promote feelings of happiness.

One of forgiveness's most beautiful gifts is that it has the power to mend relationships, which fosters deeper connections and reduces feelings of isolation. Forgiveness will shift your focus from negative experiences to positive possibilities, promoting a more optimistic view of life. Remember that forgiveness is for *you*! You are the main one who benefits when you allow yourself to forgive. You are not letting the person off the hook, so to speak, but you are freeing yourself from a lifetime of pain.

Forgiveness Is Not Weakness

No deed in the universe ever goes unpunished. This idea is represented in almost all religions and philosophies. Those who steal will be stolen from; only a much greater theft will take place. Those who cheat will be cheated on. Those who lie may never find the truth. What you put out into this world will come back to you, often tenfold—all of the good as well as all of the bad. Remember this if you ever feel like the person you are forgiving is getting away with something.

Forgiveness is often misunderstood and seen as a sign of weakness or an act of letting someone off the hook. However, true forgiveness takes strength; it's not about condoning wrong behavior or pretending that nothing happened. It is, rather, a conscious, energetic decision to let go of resentment, anger, and the desire for revenge, freeing yourself from the emotional chains that bind you to the past. This act of letting go brings immense mental and spiritual benefits, offering healing and liberation for the one who forgives. Like Gandhi said, "The weak can never forgive; forgiveness is an attribute of the strong."

The Mental Weight of Holding on to Pain

When someone wrongs you, whether through betrayal, dishonesty, or hurtful actions, the emotional pain can run deep. Often, this pain is accompanied by feelings of anger, bitterness, or even hatred. These emotions, though valid, are heavy burdens to carry. Holding on to resentment doesn't punish the offender as much as it punishes you. It keeps the wound fresh, preventing it from healing, and occupies your mental space with negativity. By holding on to grudges, you allow the actions of others to dominate your thoughts and emotional well-being. The mind in this state becomes consumed by rumination, rehearsing past hurts over and over again, forcing you to relive those anxiety-producing moments. Forgiving others can help you stay present and focused on the here and now, reducing negative thoughts about the past or creating stressful stories about the future. This repetitive mental cycle can lead to chronic stress, anxiety, and even depression. Forgiveness, on the other hand, offers a release from this mental captivity. It allows you to break free from the prison of negative emotions and regain control over your peace of mind.

Forgiveness as a Path to Inner Peace

Forgiveness creates mental clarity and tranquility. When you forgive, you free your mind from the constant replaying of hurtful memories and emotions. This act of letting go creates space for peace, replacing toxic feelings with calmness and acceptance. Inner peace, derived from forgiveness, is not dependent on the other person's actions or whether they have expressed remorse. It's a personal choice to no longer allow their actions to harm your mental or emotional well-being. In this way, forgiveness is an act of self-care, a way of prioritizing your emotional health over the desire for retribution. The mental benefits of forgiveness are also measurable. George Vaillant, a pioneer in the field of positive psychology, discovered in his studies that those who practice forgiveness experience reduced levels of anxiety, depression, and stress. They sleep better, have healthier relationships, and report an overall higher quality of life. The mind, when not burdened by negative emotions, can focus on positive pursuits, leading to greater mental clarity, creativity, and increased productivity.

Spiritual Liberation Through Forgiveness

On a spiritual level, forgiveness transcends the material or physical aspect of life and taps into something deeper. Many spiritual traditions, from Christianity to Buddhism, emphasize the transformative power of forgiveness as a path to liberation. Forgiveness aligns with the highest virtues of compassion, love, and empathy, which are all qualities that elevate the soul.

Spiritually, holding on to resentment is like chaining yourself to the very thing you wish to escape. By forgiving, you break these chains, releasing not only the other person but yourself. The act of forgiving purifies the heart, cleansing it of negative emotions like anger, hatred, and vengeance and allowing space for love, compassion, and understanding. Forgiveness aligns you with the energy of healing and grace, reconnecting you to your spiritual essence. It also fosters spiritual growth by teaching humility. In forgiving, you acknowledge your own imperfections and the fact that all humans are flawed and capable of making mistakes. This recognition deepens your sense of compassion and empathy, not only toward others but also toward yourself.

By letting go of judgment, you create space for acceptance, both of others and of life's inherent unpredictability.

The Illusion of Control

One of the reasons people hold on to resentment is the illusion of control. When someone hurts you, it can feel as though holding on to anger is a way to regain some sense of power over the situation. Yet, in truth, holding a grudge gives the other person control over *your* emotional state. You may find yourself repeatedly thinking about the offense, feeling the emotions over and over again, reliving the pain. But this only keeps you trapped in the past. Forgiveness, by contrast, is a reclaiming of your own power. It is the conscious choice to say, "I will no longer allow this situation or person to control my emotional state." In that moment of forgiveness, you regain sovereignty over your own mind and spirit. Forgiveness doesn't change the past, but it does change how you relate to it. It transforms the memory of hurt into the reality of strength and resilience.

The Healing of Relationships

Forgiveness doesn't always mean reconciliation. In some cases, it may be neither safe nor wise to rebuild the relationship. However, when it is possible and appropriate, forgiveness can be the first step toward healing and mending relationships. When you forgive, you dismantle the emotional barriers that keep you disconnected from others. Forgiveness brings understanding, allowing you to see things from the other person's perspective. It also increases your ability to empathize with others, fostering compassion and understanding. Forgiveness promotes open communication and vulnerability, which are essential ingredients for building healthy relationships. When both parties are willing to forgive, it can lead to a deepening of trust, a stronger emotional bond, and a renewed sense of connection.

Forgive Yourself

While forgiving others is essential for mental and spiritual well-being, perhaps the most challenging form of forgiveness, as I mentioned earlier, is self-forgiveness. Many people carry guilt or shame over their own past mistakes, failures, or wrong choices. They judge themselves harshly, feeling unworthy of love or success. This self-condemnation can be even more damaging than the resentment held toward others. Self-forgiveness is the recognition that you are human, and, like all humans, you are imperfect. It means acknowledging your mistakes, taking responsibility, learning from them, and then letting it go. It does not mean excusing bad behavior but rather understanding that you are not defined by your past errors.

Spiritually, self-forgiveness is an act of grace. It allows you to align with your higher self, embrace your own worth, and love yourself in spite of your imperfections. By forgiving yourself, you release the shame and guilt that weigh down your spirit, allowing you to move forward with confidence and inner peace.

Forgiveness is not a one-time event. It is an ongoing practice, one that may have many levels. Life will inevitably bring moments of hurt and betrayal, just as it will bring moments of love and joy. In this cycle, the need to forgive both others and yourself will arise repeatedly. Each time you forgive, you strengthen your ability to release, heal, and grow. The more you practice forgiveness, the easier it becomes to relinquish resentment and embrace peace. At its core, forgiveness is an act of liberation. It frees you from the mental and spiritual prisons created by holding on to anger, resentment, and pain. It allows you to reclaim your mental clarity, find inner peace, and cultivate spiritual growth. By choosing to forgive, you are choosing the freedom to live in peace, love without fear, and embrace the beauty of life with an open heart.

15

GIVE, SERVE, LOVE

Have a Happier Life by Helping Others

One of the best cures for sadness is
to go and help somebody else.
—*Kari Wells*

As parents, we are constantly giving to our children. I remember a friend of mine jokingly told me, while I was on the way to the delivery room for the first time, "Get ready—it will no longer be all about you!" Laughing, I turned to her and said, "Well, thank God for that!" I already understood that when life is all about you, you live a life that is too self-centered. Any time you take the focus off yourself and help others, you have the opportunity to live a much happier life, and, as any parent can tell you, having kids will definitely do that.

Doing something for someone else, whether it's caring for a child or doing a small random act of kindness, has numerous mental health benefits. Whether it's volunteering your time, donating money or items, or helping someone in need, performing acts of service can positively impact your emotional well-being and overall mental health.

When you do something for somebody else, you release feel-good chemicals in your brain like dopamine. According to studies by psychologists at the Cleveland Clinic, helping others can boost our happiness and mood levels, giving us a feeling of fulfillment. When we help others, we get out of our own heads and away from our own problems and personal challenges.[27]

When we do something to help others, it adds more meaning to our lives as we realize that our actions can make a positive impact on the life of somebody else. It can also increase our self-worth and happiness. In addition, it helps us feel less alone, giving us a greater sense of community and connection. This can boost our self-esteem and confidence as we feel more valued and appreciated. People who go out of their way to help others also tend to have a stronger sense of empathy and compassion.

Doing Good Feels Good

Altruism is a powerful motivator. People are genuinely driven by a desire to help others. Sometimes, individuals have personal experiences that inspire them to work for a charitable organization. They may feel a close personal connection to some of the issues the charity addresses and supporting and helping others in this way can help them heal from their past.

Helping others is so powerful that it is believed to be one of the main motivators in helping recovering alcoholics stay sober. *The Big Book of Alcoholics Anonymous*—the manual that functions as the organization's "Bible"—states that "practical experience shows nothing will so much ensure immunity from drinking as intensive work with other alcoholics [helping others stay sober]. It works when other activities fail."[28] Allowing themselves to get out of their own problems and feelings and out into the world helping others can lift the mood of an alcoholic to such a degree that they do not feel the need to drink.

Many people want to work to create a better future, not just for themselves but for society as a whole. They believe in collective action and want to play a part in solving local, international, or global challenges like climate change, racial inequality, or access to food, water, and education. When you work with a specific charity, you often meet others who share similar goals, which helps you feel like you're part of a community. Additionally, seeing the tangible results of your work can be deeply gratifying.

I always feel so good about myself when I have the opportunity to give back, and that's why I've worked with many charities in my life. Taking time to step outside your own life and issues and work with those who are less fortunate can be extremely rewarding. We all have something to give, whether it's time, a donation of items or money, or encouragement and expertise—there are many worthy causes and many ways to help.

When my children were young, we went on a family trip to Guatemala. There we discovered an organization called From Houses to Homes, which provides housing, education, and healthcare to thousands of families in rural Guatemalan communities. We worked with this organization to build a simple house for people who owned a rural piece of land but had no means of building their own home on it. In the short span of a week, thanks to this wonderful organization, we built a house for a young family that they will own for generations. This was life-changing for my kids because they'd never experienced anything like this. They were incredibly excited to go to work at eight o'clock each morning, climbing into the back of a truck and heading into the remote mountains of Guatemala to help a family build their new home.

It was a life-changing experience for all of us. Our son has since returned to build another house for a family with small children. For my children, who had grown up with so much and were living in a first world bubble, seeing true poverty helped them develop empathy and a better understanding of the world. This was crucial for them to experience during the middle school years, when most kids are incredibly self-centered. They learned from an early age that helping others is the right thing to do and also that it feels good.

Get Involved

From Houses to Homes, the charity we worked with is a grassroots organization that provides help for many Guatemalans living in extreme poverty and substandard conditions. The program, which has helped thousands of families since 2004, is structured so that volunteers, working with a team of experienced construction workers, can build an entire house from start to finish in just five days. I highly recommend this program for any family who wants to give back and educate their children about inequalities in the world. It is a beautiful, life-changing opportunity for everyone.

Many schools and colleges offer ways for students to get involved in their local community. I encourage you to get your children to research some programs and charitable organizations and get involved in one. This will help kids (and adults!) develop much-needed empathy and world awareness.

If you're not sure how to get started, think of an issue you are passionate about. Many individuals are drawn to specific charities because they feel strongly about a particular cause, such as fighting poverty, promoting education, protecting the environment, or advancing social justice. There are thousands of charities and many needy causes. Take a moment to consider what *you* care about and where you want to make a difference. If you are unable to give money, don't worry—there are many options for donating your time and talents. Charity Navigator, Guide Star, Charity Watch, and Give Well are all great resources for getting more in-depth information on possible charities to support.

Helping others is a way to help yourself. It really doesn't seem fair that one child in the world can be born with so much and another child with so little. In America, we are fortunate to have a welfare system that offers assistance to those who need it, but many countries do not have this kind of social safety net. Here in Aspen, where I currently live, there are charitable events happening almost every week for various causes, but for me, raising money for organizations that help women and children and people in Third World countries are the things I care most about.

I love supporting anything that empowers girls and women. When you change a girl, you change a generation, even a nation. There are many women's charities you can get involved in. In Atlanta, I worked with Wellspring Living, an organization that fights sex trafficking by providing domestic sex trafficking victims and those at risk, ages twelve and over, with comprehensive, trauma-informed, victim-centered recovery services through residential programs, community-based programs, and post-program support. Their residential program provides women and youth who have experienced trauma with informed care in a safe environment where participants receive education, training, and much-needed therapy.

Each time tragedy strikes around the world, whether it be from wars or natural disasters, the Red Cross and Médecins Sans Frontières (Doctors Without Borders) are always some of the first groups on the scene to offer help. The Red Cross feeds and shelters people after disaster strikes and helps individuals and communities prepare for, respond to, and recover from disasters. Additionally, they teach lifesaving skills to tens of thousands of individuals around the world. Médecins Sans Frontières (Doctors Without Borders) provides independent, impartial, medical humanitarian assistance to the people who need it most. They offer medical treatment and care for those affected by conflict, disease outbreaks, and natural and human-made disasters. Their teams deliver emergency medical aid and healthcare in more than seventy countries every day.

Amnesty International is a global human-rights organization dedicated to protecting human rights, as outlined in the Universal Declaration of Human Rights, which was created in 1961. They work tirelessly to prevent injustices and grave human rights abuses in over 150 countries and territories around the world.

Action in Africa is a fantastic organization whose founders I know personally. I have witnessed their tireless work from the ground up. They are dedicated to empowering underserved communities in Uganda by fostering sustainable development and providing essential resources such as quality education, healthcare, and community support. Founded in 2005 by a group of compassionate high school students, the organization began as a response to the challenges faced by East African communities. Today, Action in Africa serves as a pillar of support for the Nakuwadde community, operating free community centers, pop-up healthcare clinics, and partnerships with local schools. Their holistic approach ensures that children receive a high-quality education, families gain access to critical life-improving services, and the entire community is equipped to build a brighter, more self-sustaining future.

Best Buddies is a large organization dedicated to ending the social, physical, and economic isolation of the 200 million people worldwide with intellectual and developmental disabilities (IDD). Their programs empower people with IDD to form meaningful friendships with peers, secure jobs, improve communication and advocacy skills, and live independently while also offering support for their families. They have a local chapter that I love to work with, and it is wonderful to see the joy that these children exude when they get a moment to shine and be heard.

If you are still searching for a charity that speaks to you, which you want to support financially, I recommend spending time reading through the many heartbreaking stories found on GoFundMe. This incredible crowdfunding platform allows groups or organizations to campaign for their financial needs, allowing you to donate directly to the goal they have set for medical expenses, educational support, disaster relief, community projects, and other personal financial needs.

There are so many ways to help—and giving to, serving, and loving others will also help you live a happier life. I encourage you to think about what's important to you, do some research, and find a charity to support. When you take the time to get out of your own life and work to help enrich the lives of others, the whole world benefits.

RECOMMENDED CHARITABLE ORGANIZATIONS

The charities listed below all do excellent work both in the US and around the world.

- **Amnesty International**
  https://www.amnesty.org/en/
- **Action in Africa**
  https://www.actioninafrica.com
- **Best Buddies**
  https://www.bestbuddies.org
- **Doctors Without Borders**
  https://www.doctorswithoutborders.org
- **From Houses to Homes**
  https://www.fromhousestohomes.org
- **GoFundMe**
  https://www.gofundme.com
- **Wellspring Living**
  https://wellspringliving.org

16

CONCLUSION

The Fundamental Five

How you start your day is
how you live your life.
—*Louise Hay*[29]

Congratulations! You've (almost) made it to the end of this book. I hope you have found some pearls of wisdom you will take with you on your journey through life. There is a great deal of information in the world, but wisdom without action—whether that's physical action or a written, actionable plan—is merely a collection of words. All the wisdom in the world can be wasted if you fail to take action. Remember, knowing and doing are two different things. This is why I want to leave you with a list of five simple things you can start doing today, and every day, to achieve lasting joy.

In this final section, you will find a list of what I like to call "The Fundamental Five." This is a list of five simple things you can start today in order to feel more peace, more joy, and more contentment in your daily life. It's a way to apply what you've learned in the pages of this book. These suggestions are easy to follow, and they can serve as a foundation for how you live your life on a daily basis. Some of you might read these five simple things and think, *Well, duh—that's easy!* But that's precisely the point. Reading them is one thing, but *practicing* them—and incorporating them into your life on a daily basis—is where the magic happens.

Make a note of the date you start this practice and commit to doing it for *at least two weeks*. You'll find *gratitude* twice on this list. It may seem a little repetitive, especially with it being the first and last items on the list, but trust me, there is nothing that will bring more peace and more happiness into your life than practicing gratitude. Without it, no amount of money, power, or fame will bring you lasting joy. You can travel the world trying to find yourself, but until you have found gratitude, all the riches in the world will seem worthless, and you will find yourself forever trapped in the cycle of always wanting and needing more.

Without further ado, I give you The Fundamental Five:

1. **Awaken each morning with gratitude.** You get to decide how this is going to look for you. For me, it is a list I keep at my bedside, in a leather-bound

notebook. When I awaken each morning, I read the list. I sometimes get down on my knees in thanks for the many blessings I have. You can start with the list you wrote down as you worked through the chapters of this book. Then add to it so you can read it in part or in full each morning when you wake up. Create a mental copy of your list to recite on your way to work, especially if you are feeling stressed out or are stuck in traffic, and try to remember as many things as you can from this gratitude list so you can pull from it when needed.

2. **Live in the present moment.** Believe right now that you are more than your thoughts. You are a spiritual being having a human experience. So let go of the past, stop stressing about the future, and live fully in the present moment. Each time you feel yourself getting stressed, try to bring your thoughts back to the present. Do a quick meditation, working on slowing down your breathing and telling yourself that everything is okay *right now.*
3. **Create a positive and personal mantra and recite it daily.** This is something I love to keep on hand. It's like a shot of espresso for a negative mind, something that everybody should have, and it starts with "I am . . ." Make a list of all the positive statements that describe you—or that you would like to describe you. For example: *I am happy. I am loving. I am caring. I am positive. I am beautiful. I am adored. I am intelligent. I am kind. I am fierce.* Next, speak your goals as if they are your current

reality: *I am living life to the fullest. I am the leader of my team. I am happily married. I am in love. I am living in my dream home.* Keep this personal mantra in your notebook, memorize it, and change it to suit whatever you want to be as you go through the various and ever-changing chapters of your life.

4. **Do something for someone else.** It's time to get out of your head, out of your thoughts, and out of your self-absorption. Look around you. Who do you see that is less fortunate than you? Perhaps it is the unhoused person you pass every day on the street . . . or the lady who struggles with addiction and mental illness and is always ranting on the street corner . . . or your disabled coworker who finds it challenging to do things that able-bodied workers take for granted . . . or anyone you know who just can't seem to catch a break. Think about how lucky you are in comparison to many people around you. And then try to spend your day by having more compassion. Is there something you could do to help somebody else today? Maybe it's just offering a kind and encouraging word to a coworker or giving a few dollars to someone in need, but one small act of kindness can mean the world to someone.
5. **End your day with gratitude.** As you lie down to fall asleep, recite all the things you are grateful for, everything that is wonderful in your life—your health, your friends, your family, your mind, your safety or security, your good fortune, etc. If some of these things do not apply to you right now, then

find the things that do, and give thanks for those. Always choose to end your day with gratitude, focusing on your blessings and all of the things that you have.

Completing The Fundamental Five, each day, will help cultivate peace, clarity and lasting happiness. I wish for you and your loved ones all of the beautiful blessings the world has to offer, as you continue on your spiritual journey. May you walk though this journey not just seeking, but becoming the beauty and the magic that you long to find, remembering that what you seek is not hidden in the vastness around you, but revealed in the stillness within you.

GOD SPEED

ENDNOTES

1. Kenneth Kendler, "The Origin of Our Modern Concept of Depression-The History of Melancholia From 1780-1880: A Review," JAMA psychiatry, August 1, 2020, https://pubmed.ncbi.nlm.nih.gov/31995137/#:~:text=Abstract,understandably%20from%20the%20abnormal%20mood.
2. "Depression: Causes, Symptoms, Types & Treatment," Cleveland Clinic, June 2, 2025, https://my.clevelandclinic.org/health/diseases/9290-depression.
3. Jamie Cannon, "3 Victim Mentalities That Can Impede Progress," *Psychology Today*, May 16, 2022, https://www.psychologytoday.com/us/blog/stress-fracture/202205/3-victim-mentalities-can-impede-progress.
4. Viktor Frankl, *Man's Search for Meaning*, (Touchstone, 1984), pg. 86.
5. "What Is EMDR Therapy?," EMDR Institute - Eye Movement Desensitization and Reprocessing Therapy, December 3, 2024, https://www.emdr.com/what-is-emdr/#:~:text=More%20than%2030%20positive%20controlled,bring%20them%20in%20for%20therapy.

6. Ron Potter, "Opposite of Victim," Team Leadership Culture, February 8, 2022, https://www.teamleadershipculture.com/blog/opposite-victim/.
7. Byron Katie, *Loving What Is*, (Three Rivers Press, 2003).
8. "Mindfulness Can Improve Heart Health," Harvard Health, February 1, 2018, https://www.health.harvard.edu/heart-health/mindfulness-can-improve-heart-health#:~:text=A%20meditation%20practice%20supports%20your,among%20people%20without%20cardiovascular%20disease.
9. Bryan Walsh, "Does Spirituality Make You Happy?," *Time*, August 7, 2017, https://time.com/4856978/spirituality-religion-happiness/.
10. Thomas F. Crum, *Journey to Center*, (Touchstone, 1997), 89.
11. Deepak Chopra, *The Seven Spiritual Laws of Success*, 81.
12. "Gratitude," *Psychology Today*, accessed August 11, 2025, https://www.psychologytoday.com/us/basics/gratitude#:~:text=Psychologists%20find%20that%2C%20over%20time,Created%20with%20Sketch.
13. Andy Stanley, "Give Thanks: An Attitude of Gratitude," YouTube, November 23, 2020, https://www.youtube.com/watch?v=U7aneTHx2iw.
14. "Gratitude in Early Addiction Recovery: Hazelden Betty Ford," Hazelden Betty Ford Foundation, June 23, 2023, https://www.hazeldenbettyford.org/articles/gratitude-early-recovery.
15. Madhuleena Roy Chowdhury, "The Neuroscience of Gratitude and Effects on the Brain," PositivePsychology.com, April 9, 2019, https://positivepsychology.com/neuroscience-of-gratitude/.

16. "10 Malala Yousafzai Quotes to Inspire You," IWDA, September 6, 2018, https://iwda.org.au/10-of-our-favourite-malala-quotes-to-get-you-inspired/#:~:text=She's%20a%20women's%20rights%20icon,instead%20of%20flowers%20and%20butterflies.
17. "Declaration of Intention for Albert Einstein," The Library of Congress, accessed August 11, 2025, https://www.loc.gov/item/2021667583/#:~:text=Summary,a%20U.S.%20citizen%20in%201940.
18. "Biographies of the Secretaries of State: Madeleine Korbel Albright (1937–2022)," U.S. Department of State, accessed August 11, 2025, https://history.state.gov/departmenthistory/people/albright-madeleine-korbel.
19. "Meet Our Founder, Gina Murdock," LEAD WITH LOVE, accessed August 5, 2025, https://www.ileadwithlove.org/ginamurdock.
20. Wayne Dyer, "Being At Peace Rather Than Right | Wayne Dyer's Advice," YouTube, July 9, 2024, https://www.youtube.com/watch?v=r7maijM0fPQ&t=85s.
21. Joan Durrant and Ron Ensom, "Physical Punishment of Children: Lessons from 20 Years of Research," Canadian Medical Association Journal, September 4, 2012, https://pmc.ncbi.nlm.nih.gov/articles/PMC3447048/#:~:text=Physical%20punishment%20is%20associated%20with,37.
22. Kristel Alla, "What Does the Evidence Tell Us about Physical Punishment of Children?" Australian Institute of Family Studies, August 2021, https://aifs.gov.au/resources/short-articles/what-does-evidence-tell-us-about-physical-punishment-children.
23. "'The Secret to Winning Is Learning How to Lose. That Is, Learning to Bounce Back from Failure and Disappointment-Undeterred-and Continuing to Steadily March toward

Your Potential. Your Response to Failure Determines Your Capacity for Success.,'" James Clear, May 9, 2025, https://jamesclear.com/quotes/the-secret-to-winning-is-learning-how-to-lose-that-is-learning-to-bounce-back-from-failure-and-disappointment-undeterred-and-continuing-to-steadily-march-toward-your-potenti#:~:text=.

24. "The Colonial American Dream," Literary Themes for Students: The American Dream, Encyclopedia.com, last modified September 3, 2025, accessed September 19, 2025, https://www.encyclopedia.com/education/educational-magazines/colonial-american-dream..
25. Thomas Crum, *Journey to Center*, (Touchstone, 1997).
26. Deepak Chopra, *The Seven Spiritual Laws of Success*, (Amber-Allen, 2007).
27. Cleveland Clinic, "Joy in Giving Back to Your Community," Cleveland Clinic, April 22, 2025, https://newsroom.clevelandclinic.org/2024/12/03/joy-in-giving-back-to-your-community.
28. Alcoholics Anonymous, *The Big Book*, (AAWS, 2001).
29. Louise Hay, "Morning Meditation and Affirmations with Louise Hay Start Your Day Right," YouTube, March 13, 2024, https://www.youtube.com/watch?v=HIUB0A54lDU.